In Search of Wonder

Contributors

LYNN ANDERSON, minister in Dallas, Texas, for over thirty-five years, received his doctorate from Abilene Christian University in 1990. He has written several books including *Finding the Heart to Go On, Freshness for the Far Journey, If I Really Believe Why Do I Have These Doubts?, Heaven Came Down,* and *Navigating the Winds of Change.*

MAX LUCADO holds a B.A. and M.A. from Abilene Christian University. He currently serves as a minister of the Oak Hills Church of Christ in San Antonio and can be heard on "UpWords" radio program daily. His books include *A Gentle Thunder, The Applause of Heaven, In the Eye of the Storm, He Still Moves Stones, And the Angels Were Silent,* and *When God Whispers Your Name.*

MIKE COPE, minister for twelve years, holds a M.Th. from Harding Graduate School of Religion. He is a highly sought after conference speaker, the author of *Living in Two Worlds, Righteousness Inside Out, Teens in Two Worlds,* and *One Holy Hunger,* and coeditor of *Wineskins* magazine.

RANDALL J. HARRIS is a Ph.D. candidate at Syracuse University, an instructor in the Bible Department at David Lipscomb University, and coauthor of *Second Incarnation.* He also serves as a minister in Nashville, Tennessee.

RUBEL SHELLY holds a M.A. and M.Th. from Harding Graduate School of Religion and a M.A. and Ph.D. from Vanderbilt University. He has served as a minister in Nashville for over fifteen years and has taught at David Lipscomb University and Vanderbilt University School of Medicine. He has authored more than twenty books and is coeditor of *Wineskins* magazine.

HAROLD SHANK holds a Ph.D. from Marquette University and serves as a minister in Memphis, Tennessee. He is the author of *Loosening Your Grip: Letting Go and Living in True Security.* Shank is also on the editorial board of *Twenty-First Century Christian* magazine.

JACK REESE is the chair of the Department of Graduate Bible and Ministry at Abilene Christian University and professor of preaching and worship. Reese holds a Ph.D. in theology from the University of Iowa School of Religion and is a well-known writer of numerous articles for Christian publications.

In Search of Wonder

A Call to Worship Renewal

Edited by
Dr. Lynn Anderson

MAX LUCADO

LYNN ANDERSON

RUBEL SHELLY

MIKE COPE

RANDALL HARRIS

JACK REESE

HAROLD SHANK

HOWARD
PUBLISHING CO.
West Monroe, Louisiana

Our purpose at Howard Publishing is:

- *Instructing* believers toward a deeper faith in Jesus
  Christ
- *Inspiring* holiness in the lives of believers
- *Instilling* hope in the hearts of struggling people
  everywhere

Because he's coming again

Howard Publishing Co., Inc.,
3117 North 7th Street, West Monroe, Louisiana 71291-2227

In Search of Wonder
© 1995 by Howard Publishing Co., Inc.
All rights reserved. Published 1995
Printed in the United States of America

Second printing 1996

Cover Design by LinDee Loveland
Manuscript Editing by Philis Boultinghouse

ISBN 1-878990-41-1

Scripture quotations not otherwise marked are from the New International Version, © 1973, 1978, 1984 by International Bible Society.
Used by permission Zondervan Bible Publishers.

Contents

96271

Introduction

DR. LYNN ANDERSON

Dan had never experienced anything like this. His thick fingers nervously brushed through his black hair as he tried to hold back the tears that fell from his eyes and the emotions that welled up in his heart. He leaned over to the friend who had brought him to this "event" and whispered, "When I go home, I'm going to be a changed man."

Carol had come against her will. Shannon, a friend from work, had been so persistent that Carol just couldn't say no. As she stood among the crowd of people, she remembered standing in front of the mirror just an hour earlier, brushing her wavy blond hair and dressing her deep brown eyes for this morning's event. Begrudgingly, she had climbed out of the bed of a man who was not her husband and whom she did not love to meet Carol here. But now she was hugging Carol with genuine affection, and between her heavy sobs, she made the firm commitment never to return to that man or his bed again.

Paul and Susan arrived wearing dull, unexpectant expressions. This all-American couple came expecting a predictably mind-numbing ordeal of little benefit and even less enjoyment. They were from out of town and were simply visiting Susan's mother. This boring session would soon be over, and they could head home. But as the proceedings began, surprise replaced their boredom. Then, as the morning unfolded, their faces lit up with joy and satisfaction. They held each other's hands and the hands of those sitting next to them. Paul placed his arm around Susan's shoulder, and they looked into each other's eyes. Without saying a word, they knew the lights had been turned back on in their lives.

You are probably wondering what special occasion these people were part of. What special event affected their lives so positively and dramatically?

It was simply a Sunday morning worship service at a local church—but it was vibrant, authentic, meaning-ful—a service that linked their hearts with the almighty God and his transforming power. Can worship really be a history-making event where participants are renewed and molded into the likeness of God? Do churches like this really exist? The answer is *yes*. While such churches are not exactly typical, their numbers are growing. For these churches, worship is not about tradition and rou-tine; worship is about God—his power, his glory, his will, and his plans for men and women everywhere.

Some call efforts to revitalize worship a "praise craze"; they fear that authentic worship will get lost in marketing and entertainment or that the church will lose contact with its roots. Admittedly, some change is superficial—mere tinkering with lights, microphones, and audiovisuals. But the biggest and most important things happening in worship renewal are far more substantive than mere bells and whistles. Massive numbers of Christians long for more meaningful worship. They will not be satisfied with anything less than authentic pursuit of God—in both public and personal times of worship. These people are in search of wonder. They long for worship with more theological content and less predictability, more God and less us, more participation and less rote ritual. They want fresh expressions of praise in the language of today; yet they do not want to cut themselves off from the past.

In 1992, Hope Network sponsored a church leaders' seminar—A Church That Connects I—which advocated change in some of our systems and formats for reaching and nurturing this rapidly shifting culture. This led to A Church That Connects II, which articulated principles of responsible change management, and ultimately to a book titled *Navigating the Winds of Change,* published by Howard Publishing Company.

In the wake of Connect II, we heard a growing request among attendees for help with theological foundations in worship renewal, lest the changes become mere fiddling with forms.

The response to these requests culminated in the 1994 A Church That Connects III and in the book you now hold in your hands. I firmly believe God's hand was at work in bringing this book together. Six of today's finest Christian scholars, communicators, and opinion leaders who, above all, share a passion for God, worked with me to compose the chapters that make up this relevant and important book. All contributors share an intense love for biblical teaching on worship, all live their lives "in search of wonder," and all are eager to contribute toward a sound biblical theology of worship articulated in layman's language.

Because of the caliber of men I worked with and the topic we addressed, I thoroughly enjoyed the task of rough-editing this volume. Hats off in gratitude to the contributing writers:

- Max Lucado, well-known Christian writer, radio voice, and San Antonio minister

- Mike Cope, Texas minister, writer, and widely sought after conference speaker

- Randall J. Harris, minister and professor, David Lipscomb University

- Dr. Rubel Shelly, Nashville minister, writer, and adjunct professor, Vanderbilt University

- Dr. Harold Shank, Memphis minister and adjunct professor, Harding Graduate School of Religion

- Dr. Jack R. Reese, dean of Graduate Department of Religious Studies, Abilene Christian University

A huge bouquet of roses to Philis Boultinghouse of Howard Publishing Company who has poured her soul and her excellent professional skills into the final edit of this book.

Together we offer it to you, dear readers, who too are "in search of wonder." We understand, of course, that this is only a beginning; yet we hope this step toward a theology of worship for today's church will assist you and your circle of believers toward a more authentic and consistent encounter with God. To him be the glory.

DR. LYNN ANDERSON

◆

To Endless Years the Same

A Definition
of Worship

CHAPTER ONE

Before the hills in order stood,
    Or earth received her frame,
From everlasting Thou art God,
    To endless years the same.[1]

This verse from Isaac Watt's classic hymn "O God, Our Help in Ages Past" reminds us that God has been around a long time. Eternally, in fact! And human beings have worshiped him since the days of Eden.

The conversation began innocuously, with a simple question about drinking water. Then it moved to Jews, then to men and to husbands, then to prophets and temples. Finally she got around to the industrial strength question—about God! She was actually asking the same question we are asking—just phrased in a different way, "Where are we supposed to worship God? In your temple or on our mountain?" (see John 4:20–24). In other words, "Where do I find God? How do I worship him?"

Jesus gave her a strange answer, "You Samaritans worship what you do not know. We worship what we do know, for salvation is from the Jews." With this answer, he dropped a reminder of the long, long roots of Yahweh worship.

Continuity between the Old and New Testaments

Jesus reminded the woman at the well, and us, that a full and balanced biblical panorama of worship is painted in a radical continuity between the Old and New Testaments. This stands, of course, in contrast to the radical discontinuity many of us have been taught.

2

Where Do We Learn of Worship?

The New Testament texts, if taken by themselves, leave us with an impoverished view of worship. After all, the Bible of the New Testament church was the Old Testament! Centuries of revelation and tradition on worship shaped the understanding of the New Testament church—images of the transcendent God, encounters with the Holy One, the Psalms. And when New Testament writers referred to worship, they assumed that their readers already held the rich view of worship which is "from the Jews." Consequently, New Testament writers spill very little ink articulating the core nature of worship.

Early New Testament worship reflected synagogue assemblies, not the rich environment of the temple. The synagogue was a school, a place of teaching the word, a place of ideas; whereas the temple was a place of full-blown praise and exaltation. Temple and synagogue experiences together shape the whole biblical picture of worship.

Actually, discussion of worship in the New Testament deals primarily with correctives—concerning things that had gone wrong in the church assemblies; it deals very little with worship per se. Thus, it takes both testaments to give us the whole, balanced picture of worship. Synagogue and temple, teaching and praise— a radical continuity throughout the whole Bible.

Some may object, "But, what of the division between the testaments I've been taught most of my life? I thought the Old Testament was done away with. What about the King James version of 2 Timothy 2:15, 'Study to shew thyself approved unto God . . . rightly dividing the word of truth?'"

Many have taken the 2 Timothy passage to mean that correct Bible study divides the Scriptures into two radically discontinuous theologies. Or stated bluntly, "Chop the Bible in half. Leave the first half behind. We are now under the New Testament."

Neglecting the Old Testament has caused some of us to distort some parts of the New Testament, resulting in (among other things) a muddled theology of worship. By way of illustration, one aged preacher, whom I love and respect, recently lamented to me, "Psalm 23 should have been in the New Testament. It's a shame such a beautiful notion got left in the Old Testament." He implied that somehow, just by being in the Old Testament, the psalm loses significance.

What Has Changed?

Some things are definitely different this side of the cross. Our means of approaching God is now through Jesus. As our new priest, he replaced faulty human priesthood. His once-for-all sacrifice replaced the futility of repeated animal sacrifice, which could never take away sin (Heb. 10:4).

And, in some senses, the law was "nailed up." Christ "canceled the written code, with its regulations, that was against us and that stood opposed to us; he took it away, nailing it to the cross" (Col. 2:14). Jesus abolished "in his flesh the law with its commandments and regulations" (Eph. 2:15). The "law was put in charge to lead us to Christ that we might be justified by faith. Now that faith has come, we are no longer under the . . . law" (Gal. 3:24–25).

As a means of achieving salvation, the law was nailed up. Fact is, no one is saved by law keeping. Not then. Not now. Jesus nailed up the notion that one could be saved by keeping the commandments of the law.

The ceremonial expression of the law was nailed up, with its human priesthood, its animal sacrifices, its oblations and rituals. And the law, as an external and institutional means of identifying God's people, was nailed up. No longer are God's people designated as "the ones who keep the rules of the old law" (specifically circumcision). In a very clear sense, the old law no longer stands in judgment over us.

What Has Stayed the Same?

But, on the other hand, the core truth of Old Testament teaching still stands. Theology (our understanding of God) is still shaped by the Old Testament as well as the New. Although Christians are not saved by meeting the standards of the law, the Ten Commandments are still essentially and fundamentally true because they describe and express the nature of an eternal God. They lay out the foundation of a lifestyle lived out in relationship with God. Of course, we now have a far more profound concept of the Sabbath than a mere Saturday's rest, but the will of God is still basically the same. Paul said, "So then, the law is holy, and the commandment is holy, righteous and good" (Rom. 7:12), and "We know that the law is good if one uses it properly" (1 Tim. 1:8).

God is still the same God: his nature has not changed.

We are still the same needy, sinful creatures. That hasn't changed.

Salvation is still only by God's grace through faith— always has been. It was for Abraham, and it still is for us. That hasn't changed.

And the authentic cry of humble hearts is still of central importance with God. That has not changed.

Jesus—the Fulfillment of the Law

The law was not abolished; it was *fulfilled.* Jesus is the fulfillment of the law. He said,

> Do not think that I have come to abolish the Law or the Prophets; I have not come to abolish them but to fulfill them. I tell you the truth, until heaven and earth disappear, not the smallest letter, not the least stroke of a pen, will by any means disappear from the Law until everything is accomplished. Anyone who breaks one of the least of these commandments and teaches others to do the same will be called least in the kingdom of heaven. (Matt. 5:17–19)

However, the law is packaged differently for us this side of the cross. Listen to Jesus, "In everything, do to others what you would have them do to you, for this sums up the Law and the Prophets" (Matt. 7:12). When we treat others the way we want to be treated, we are "doing the law." Jesus also said, "'Love the Lord your God with all your heart and with all your soul and with all your mind.' This is the first and greatest commandment. And the second is like it: 'Love your neighbor as yourself.' All the Law and the Prophets hang on these two commandments" (Matt. 22:37–40). Loving God and neighbor is "doing the law."

Doing the law is not rule-keeping; doing the law is relationship with God through Jesus. And he, living in us, lives out the will of God in our lives. Paul the apostle said, "The law of the Spirit of life set me free from the law of sin and death. . . . in order that the righteous requirements of the law might be fully met in us, who do not live according to the sinful nature but according to the Spirit" (Rom. 8:2, 4).

The Holy Spirit, living in us, fills us with new power to work the law in us. Thus, Jesus empowers us to live in harmony with the will of God though the strength of the Holy Spirit. The Spirit both deals with sin, "by the Spirit you put to death the misdeeds of the body" (Rom. 8:13), and fills us with the fruit of the Spirit, "love, joy, peace, patience, kindness, goodness, faithfulness, gentleness and self-control. Against such things there is no law" (Gal. 5:22–23).

No. The old law is not done away with. Rather it is fulfilled in Jesus to be lived out in Christians by the power of the spirit.

In this way, the eternal and holy law of an almighty and changeless God is internalized in our minds and hearts. "This is the covenant I will make with them after that time, says the Lord. I will put my laws in their hearts, and I will write them on their minds" (Heb. 10:16, cf. Jer. 31:33). The heart of the worshiper is the central ingredient in acceptable worship.

Doing the law is not rule-keeping, but relationship with God through Jesus.

Like Jesus explained to the woman at the Samaritan well, "A time is coming and has now come when the true worshipers will worship the Father in spirit and truth, for they are the kind of worshipers the Father seeks. God is spirit, and his worshipers must worship in spirit and in truth" (John 4:23–24).

There is far more to the Old Testament than the law. The Old Testament is loaded with revelation about God and with revelation about man. The Old Testament gives God's account of the God/man relationship. This rich heritage shapes us and gives us discernment into ourselves and our worship of God.

Thus, I boldly assert: Worship is essentially the same in both Old and New Testaments. The Bible is radically continuous, and both Old and New Testaments contribute to a full and balanced theology of worship. Since we are the same and God is the same and truth is the same, let's go back and look at the whole Bible as we learn how to worship.

Worship as Defined through Both Testaments

1. Worship Is about God

First and foundationally, through both Old and New Testaments, *worship is about God,* not about us! Worship is fundamentally praise: it is our response to God for who he is and what he has done.

Worship is fundamentally praise: it is our response to God for who he is and what he has done.

Two Old Testament Hebrew verbs spell out the heart of worship: *hallel* and *gada.* These words mean "praise," "thank," "bless," or "worship." Or in the English of today, they would mean something like, "Hooray! Hooray for God!" *Hallel* then picks up the name of God (Yahweh) and forms our word *Hallel Yahweh,* or *Hallelujah,* which simply means "Praise God." However, the word *hallelujah,* meaning "praise the Lord" or "give thanks to the Lord," is a preliminary phrase leading to the "main event" expression of who God is and what he has done. "Praise the Lord" is a preliminary or a call to praise, an urging to praise, or a profession of a desire to praise. It is the "because of" or "for" preceding the *main event*. An example of the main event might be, "His mercies endure forever." Praise the Lord because . . . Praise the Lord because he created the world or because his love endures forever. One clear example of the preliminary/main event sequence is the repetition in Psalm 136:

> Give thanks to the Lord, for he is good. *(preliminary)*
>
> His love endures forever. *(main event)*
>
> Give thanks to the God of gods. *(preliminary)*
>
> His love endures forever. *(main event)*
>
> To him who alone does great wonders, *(preliminary)*
>
> His love endures forever. *(main event)*

God has countless "main event" characteristics for which we praise him. Two examples are his holiness and his presence among us.

God's Holiness

God's holiness elicits worship and awe. God is frequently imaged in Scripture as "the Holy One of Israel": "There is no one holy like the Lord; there is no one besides you" (1 Sam. 2:2); "Who is it you have insulted and blasphemed? Against whom have you raised your voice and lifted your eyes in pride? Against the Holy One of Israel!" (2 Kings 19:22); "Our shield belongs to the Lord, our king to the Holy One of Israel" (Ps. 89:18).

Holy means "other," "beyond," "separate"—the opposite of "common" or "profane."

Isaiah pictured God as "seated on a throne, high and exalted . . . the train of his robe [filling] the temple" (Isa.

6:1). In Isaiah's vision, God was surrounded by flying six-winged seraphim, who covered their feet and their faces and cried out, "Holy, holy, holy is the Lord Almighty; the whole earth is full of his glory" (Isa. 6:3). In Exodus, his holiness shook the mountains and filled the earth with fire, smoke, thunder, lightning, and trumpet blast. The earth trembled and the people fell back in fear, because even if an animal touched the mountain, it would surely be put to death (Exod. 19:12–13). The writer of Hebrews calls us to "worship God acceptably with reverence and awe, for our 'God is a consuming fire'" (Heb. 12:28).

This sense of fearsome wonder before a holy God fills both testaments, but is dangerously lacking in much of current Western church life. My friend, Joseph Shullam, helped me see this. While we traveled in Israel, Joseph filled my heart and head with a fresh and powerful Mid-Eastern Jewish perspective of messianic faith. On one day's travels, we passed by the traditional site of the death of Uzzah, who stretched out his hand to steady the ark of God when it nearly tumbled from an ox cart. For this act of careless irreverence, God struck the man dead on the spot (2 Sam. 6). So I asked Joseph, "From a Jewish perspective, why do you think God was so tough on Uzzah?"

Joseph looked at me as if I had personally offended him and retorted, "For the Jews, this is an inappropriate question. We do not ask God why he does anything. He is God, that's why. And we are not God. But if the Jews were to ask a question it would not likely be, 'Why did Uzzah get zapped?' but, 'How come the rest of us get off?' We all deserve to die!"

What a sobering, but dead-accurate, perspective.

I once heard Scott Peck recount the ancient Hassidic legend of Rabbi Malaki. This eager and devout rabbi prayed fervently and persistently, "Oh, Adonai, please reveal to me your true name so that I may know it even as the angels know it." Morning after morning, Malaki raised this petition.

Finally, Adonai honored the old rabbi's request, whereupon Malaki fled and hid under his bed, yelping like a frightened animal and begging Adonai to help him forget the True Name.

God's Presence among Us

God is a bewildering and wonderful paradox. Although holy and altogether "other," he has come *into our midst!* Hear this mega-oxymoron: "For I am God, and not man—the Holy One *among you*" (Hos. 11:9); "Shout aloud and sing for joy, people of Zion, for great is the Holy One of Israel *among you*" (Isa. 12:6).

"God is our refuge and strength, an ever-present help in trouble. . . . The Lord Almighty is *with us*" (Ps. 46:1, 7a). "What other nation is so great as to have their gods near them the way the Lord our God is *near us* whenever we pray to him?" (Deut. 4:7). This is a great mystery: otherness, transcendence, incomprehensibility is in our midst. He is here, beside you, right now, wherever you are sitting while you read these words. But this mystery is exactly what we believe. In fact, the first name the New Testament gives to Jesus our Lord and King is *Immanuel,* which means, "God with us."

God's presence in our midst is all the more amazing when we consider who God is in contrast with who we are. We are sinners. We are lost. We are helpless. We are hopeless. We deserve to die! "All have sinned and fall short of the glory of God" (Rom. 3:23), and "The wages of sin is death" (Rom. 6:23). This is why Isaiah, when face to face with the Holy, Holy, Holy One cried out,

"Woe to me! I am ruined! For I am a man of unclean lips, and I live among a people of unclean lips, and my eyes have seen the King, the Lord Almighty" (Isa. 6:5). And only after God dispatched an angel who touched Isaiah's lips with a live coal from the altar is Isaiah assured that his "guilt is taken away and [his] sin atoned for" (Isa. 6:7). Only then does he dare present himself for God's purposes. And only then are his motives pure enough to endure in a ministry that, from a human perspective, looks like an exercise in futility. Worship drives Isaiah's ministry.

God's presence in our midst is all the more amazing when we consider who God is in contrast with who we are.

Possibly one reason we subconsciously resist an intimate approach to God, while at the same time longing for him, is that we feel a haunting sense of our guiltiness, even when we are in denial of it.

H. G. Wells told the story of a fictitious New England bishop who was revered for his sensitivity and wisdom. People freely told him their troubles, and he would usually ask, "Have you prayed about it?" He had discovered that if that question was asked in just the right tone, it seemed to settle things a bit.

However, the bishop never prayed much himself. He felt no need for prayer. He had things all wrapped up in a tight package, until one day his life tumbled in. He found himself so overwhelmed that he decided to take his own advice and pray.

On Saturday evening he entered the cathedral, went to the front, knelt on the crimson carpet, and folded his hands before the altar. He could not help but think how childlike he was. Then he began to pray, "Oh, God . . . "

Suddenly a voice, crisp and business-like, boomed out from somewhere above him, "Well, what is it?"

On the next day, when the worshipers came to the Sunday service, they found the bishop sprawled face down on the crimson carpet. When they turned him over, they discovered he was stone dead, with lines of horror still etched on his face.

How chillingly relevant. Many of us who talk a great deal about God would be scared to death if we saw him face to face. And we ought to be. Isaiah was. So was every Bible person who found himself or herself in his terrible presence. For he is holy, and we are defiled. What a miracle that the Holy One of Israel should choose to be in our midst! Thus, worship is our response to him—not only for who he is, but also for what he has done.

This leads naturally to our second observation about worship across the centuries.

2. Worship Is about Deliverance

Through both testaments, the fundamental and major theme of worship is deliverance. "Give thanks to the Lord. Praise his name for he has delivered." Of course, there are many deliverances for which God is praised. Some of these are only "little" deliverances. One example of a little deliverance would be wandering Bedouins praising God for delivering them from thirst and starvation while lost in the desert: "They cried out to the Lord in their trouble, and he delivered them from their distress. He led them . . . to a city where they could settle" (Ps. 107:6–7). Certainly, the Lord also blesses his children with deliverance today; and the only appropriate response is praise.

However, the central deliverances in both testaments are "big" deliverances. In the Old Testament, the big deliverance is the Exodus—the deliverance from slavery to the Egyptians. "For the Lord brought you out of Egypt with his mighty hand" (Exod. 13:9). Thus, at the heart of Israel's worship was the Passover feast by which they worshiped "God our deliverer."

Deliverance is fundamental to New Testament worship as well. However, the big deliverance in the New Testament is the deliverance from slavery to sin, through the cross of Jesus Christ. The Old Testament Passover adds vivid imagery to the New Testament deliverance celebration, the Lord's Supper. Jesus transfers the meaning of the Old Testament deliverance feast, the Passover bread and wine, into the bread and wine of the Communion, which commemorates our deliverance in the cross of Christ.

The theme of deliverance is a major thread that runs all the way through the worship of both testaments. A holy God came into the midst of a sin-enslaved people to deliver us and to make us his own beloved children. Thus, worship, in both testaments, is mostly praise.

3. Worship Is Usually Set in the Assembly

Throughout both testaments, the usual worship setting is the assembly. No, worship is not merely addressing words or thoughts to God in an assembly. Worship includes the totality of life offered to God. Both testaments say so. Old Testament examples would include Joshua 24:15, "As for me and my household, we will serve [worship] the Lord." By this, Joshua did not mean "we will show up at the synagogue every Saturday."

Rather, he affirmed that "the whole of our lives will be yielded up to God."

Again in Isaiah 1:15–17, "Even if you offer many prayers, I will not listen. Your hands are full of blood; wash and make yourselves clean. . . . Stop doing wrong, learn to do right! Seek justice, encourage the oppressed. Defend the cause of the fatherless, plead the case of the widow." In other words, vertical words of worship are meaningless if they are not matched by worship as a lifestyle of compassion and holiness.

Again, in the New Testament, Paul urges the Romans, "Offer your bodies as living sacrifices—this is your spiritual act of worship" (Rom. 12:1). And Jesus explained, "If you are offering your gift at the altar and there remember that your brother has something against you, leave your gift there in front of the altar. First go and be reconciled to your brother; then come and offer your gift" (Matt. 5:23–24). Both Jesus and Paul are saying that all of life offered up to God is spiritual worship. When a farmer plows a straight furrow or a business person cuts a straight deal, or when any Christian does an act of compassion, justice, or mercy, each is an act of worship, if done to honor God.

Vertical words of worship are meaningless if they are not matched by worship as a lifestyle of compassion and holiness.

Individual Christians are also private, personal "vertical" worshipers. In fact, if you are not a private worshiper, even though you may attend church regularly, you will not likely be a public worshiper. I have often heard my friend Paul Faulkner say, "Trying to worship publicly if you are not a private worshiper is sort of like the dry heaves—trying to bring up something you don't have in you!"

Yet, through both testaments, public worship in the assembly is the centerpiece of worship and praise for the people of God. God is with his people in a special way in their assemblies.

The Psalms were written to be read publicly. In fact, a case could be made that most of the Bible was meant to be read publicly. The early church had no Xerox machines. So when a letter came from Paul, Christians would simply gather around, and someone would read that letter publicly in the assembly of the church.

When they sang psalms, in Old or New Testament times, they did so in the assembly of Israel or in the gathering of the church. What was unique about Israel's worship was not found in her rituals. Other ancient cultures practiced rites similar to the Sabbath, used elements similar to unleavened bread, and celebrated feasts similar to the Passover, New Moon, Harvest, and New Year. In Israel, rites were significant, not because of the ceremony, but because of the presence of the Holy One of Israel. The fact that God was actually *in their midst* is what was unique about Israel's worship, and his presence was symbolized by the very place of worship, whether it was the tabernacle or the temple. The Holy Place and the Holy of Holies declared the presence of God in their midst.

In the book of Hebrews (chaps. 9 and 10), we are told that Jesus' crucifixion ushers us into the Holy of Holies—the center of Old Testament worship. And in today's assemblies, a sinner may hear a prophetic message that makes sense, and thus he falls down and worships God, exclaiming, "God is really among you!" (1 Cor. 14:25).

This is why Christians who are urged to "draw near to God with a sincere heart in full assurance of faith" are also urged "not [to] give up meeting together," but to "spur one another on toward love and good deeds," because in the assemblies they would "encourage one another" (Heb. 10:22, 24–25). Or to paraphrase Paul, they would speak to one another in songs and teach one another in songs as they sang and made music in their hearts to God (Eph. 5:19, Col. 3:16). God is uniquely in our midst in worship assemblies.

4. Worship Includes Both Human Expression and Human Experience

Throughout both testaments, worship includes both human expression and human experience. By expression we mean what we *say* about or to God. By experience we mean what we *feel* because of the presence and power of God. Or, to put it differently, worship includes both teaching (synagogue influence), that is listening to God and speaking God's word, and praise (temple influence), that is talking and singing to God.

Human *expression* is vertical, God-directed language in praise and prayer. When we worship God, we human beings express ideas of adoration and thanksgiving. We express *hallels* and *gadas* to God that convey intelligible content. Paul vowed, "In the church I would rather speak five intelligible words . . . than ten thousand words in a tongue" (1 Cor. 14:19).

But worship also includes human *experience*, or the horizontal, personal feelings of the worshiper. In worship, we feel something—exuberance, gratitude, joy, awe, penitence, wonder, love, and praise. We feel these things because we are sensitive to the presence and nature of God. As the psalmist said, "I *rejoiced* with those who said to me, 'Let us go to the house of the Lord'" (Ps. 122:1). This worshiper felt something.

Both the expression and experience of praise involve the total person—the whole being: head, hands, and heart.

Head Worship

First, the head is involved—the intellectual part of the worshiper that speaks intelligible words. We sing and pray with understanding, or with the mind (1 Cor. 14:15). Worshipers think rational thoughts about God and express information to God. Walter Brueggemann, in his book *Israel's Praise,* reminds us that when we verbalize content about God and to God, we are literally "building our world."[2] We are shaping our reality; we are adjusting the lens though which we look at everything; we are setting out our identity before God and each other. When we sing the national anthem, we redefine ourselves as Americans. In a similar way, by saying the head things to and about God, we define ourselves as God followers.

Heart Worship

Second, the heart, or the emotional part of a person, is involved in worship. Feelings of joy, celebration, grief, repentance, pain, and, yes, even sometimes anger are expressed in worship. (If we cannot honestly take our anger to God, pray tell, where then can we take it?)

Hands Worship

Third, the hands or body—the physical dimension— is also involved in worship. The Bible fleshes out worship with some very physical verbs. We "kneel before the Lord our Maker" (Ps. 95:6), and "shout for joy to the Lord" (Ps. 100:1), and "clap [our] hands" (Ps. 47:1), and "raise holy hands" (Isa. 1:15; 1 Tim. 2:8). Some "fall down and worship him" (1 Cor. 14:25; Ezek. 1; Rev. 5:14). (I cannot help but reflect at this moment, "When was the last time I landed on my face before God in worship?") David even "danced before the Lord." The whole body is involved at times.

Somewhere back there we became paranoid of the physical and emotional dimensions of worship. No doubt our concern began for good reasons. We did not want to cut ourselves adrift from the secure moorings of objective, revealed truth. But the more cerebral we became, the more we tended to fear what some call "touchy-feely" kinds of things. Of course, there is a danger in overdoing the physical and emotional aspects, but the cerebral dimension is only one-third of biblical worship! Some of us have backed so far away from the ditch of emotionalism that we have gotten entangled in the fence of legalism and cold ritual. Today's church, I am convinced, is in far more danger of having swelled heads, shrunken hearts, and feeble bodies in

Some of us have backed so far away from the ditch of emotionalism that we have gotten entangled in the fence of legalism and cold ritual.

worship than we are of being overly emotional and subjective. God made the whole human being, and the whole person is involved in worship throughout both Old and New Testaments.

5. Worship Is Contemporary

In both testaments, the most authentic worship to
God is the most contemporary. According to the *American Heritage Dictionary, contemporary* means: 1. Belong-
ing to the same period of time. 2. Of about the same age.
3. Current.

We have already seen that worship is a human response to the majesty of God. So, by contemporary worship I mean human response to the majesty of God expressed in language and forms appropriate to the time
and place. Both biblically and historically, authentic
worship is best expressed in the natural, heart-language
of the worshiper in his or her own culture.

The earliest Old Testament worship of Almighty Je-
hovah God was expressed in forms contemporary to the
worshiper and relevant to the culture. As previously
stated, altars, priests, sacred places, animal sacrifices,
and holy days surrounding historical and seasonal
events did not originate with the Hebrews. Those forms
of worship were not unique to Israel, but were common
among many pagan cult worshipers. The significant
difference between Hebrew and pagan worship was not
in the style or forms of worship but in the God worshiped. Yahweh is the only true and living God.

In New Testament times, the worship of the early
church was not uniform in style across all cultures.
Communication styles differed from Jerusalem to
Athens. Meeting times and locations and styles differed
from Jerusalem to Ephesus to Troas to Rome. Qualities
for leaders differed from sophisticated, urban Ephesus
to backwoods, semirural Crete. It was God's genius for
the church that it can be true to God, yet express itself in
worship so as to connect with all cultures of all times,
instead of being locked into one people in one era.

Which New Testament style should we imitate today? The Jewish churches? The early Jewish churches expressed worship in worship styles of Jewish culture in that day: the synagogue format. This was the "contemporary worship style" in those early, first-century Jewish settings—a school model, minus temple celebration. Their liturgy and music would indeed sound strange today. Scripture readings were sung; but since there were no songbooks or standard musical score, the leader would sing a line of a psalm, improvising his tune, and the congregation would respond, repeating the line and echoing the leader's tune. With standard psalms, the leader might sing the first verse and the congregation respond with the second, and so on.

Everything, however, was improvisational. Not until relatively modern times was music written down and the form locked in place with a definite melody line and harmony. In fact, the chord structure and scale that we use today wasn't fully developed until the seventeenth century.

Or should we imitate the Gentile churches? As the church moved into Graeco-Roman Gentile cultures, worship styles began to change. Different formats emerged. No longer was the worship assembly as heavily influenced by the synagogue or temple style. For example, the preaching and teaching were done in different languages. The formats changed, too. There was a riverside church at Philippi, a schoolhouse church in Ephesus, and house churches in Rome. The issues addressed in the churches differed from culture to culture as well. At Jerusalem, the church battled over circumcision and kosher food, while Corinth had questions about fornication and meat offered to idols. In fact, Paul urged that the church communicate in culturally relevant styles. He said worship must be offered not only in the right spirit, but in an understandable fashion (1 Cor. 14:15–19). And Paul himself was willing to be enormously culturally flexible, even to "become all things to all men" in order to win them (1 Cor. 9:22).

Still later, the church took on the "contemporary" style of having church buildings, a common religious format begun after Constantine. Music shifted away from Jewish sound and melodies, which did not speak to the Greek heart. Clement of Alexandria noticed this as early as A.D. 205.[3]

Today, as in every era, if worship is to be authentically owned and offered by its generation, it best be expressed in the heart language of the worshiper. As Rubel Shelly says in chapter 4 of this book, "If worship is not relevant, it is not biblical."

6. Worship Begins with a Hungry Heart

In both testaments, although God is the object of worship, the human heart is the issue of worship. Many of us were taught in childhood to quote 1 Samuel 16:7, "Man looks at the outward appearance, but the Lord looks at the heart." The heart of worship is worship from the heart. "Love the Lord your God with all your heart" (Deut. 6:5). "Search me, O God, and know my heart" (Ps. 139:23). Jesus' sober warning still rings in our ears, "These people honor me with their lips, but their hearts are far from me" (Matt. 15:8). God doesn't want our torrent of words, unless they come from our hearts: hearts warmed by the love of God . . . hearts transfixed by the majesty of God . . . hearts falling in a holy hush at the awesome holiness of God . . . hearts bursting with jubilant praise at the goodness of God . . . hearts hungry to know God and willing to be broken over things that break the heart of God.

This brings us back to the conversation at the Samaritan well. Like many of us, this woman was confused. Our questions echo hers: "Where do I go to find God? In what holy place? Which group is made up of true worshipers? What "holy huddle" should I be a part of? If I find the right temple—the Holy House—will I find God there? Or do I need to find the correct mountain—the Hallowed Hill? If I find the proper ritual—the Heavenly Hocus Pocus—will I then connect with God? If I get my life in Moral Order will I find God? If I manage marriage better and build a Happy Home, will that impress God? But look at me! What hope do I have of being righteous enough to connect with God?"

If worship is to be authentically owned and offered by its generation, it best be expressed in the heart language of the worshiper.

Jesus looked into the heart of this woman. In spite of the way she had been misused by many human beings and even though she had wandered into a chain of destructive choices, Jesus knew that deep down in her heart, she had never lost her hunger for God, never given up her search. In so many words, he said, "Listen. It's not like that. Worship is not finding the Hallowed Hill or the Holy House or the Heavenly Hocus Pocus. It is not even in achieving Moral Order or in building a Happy Home. Those things won't get you to God. Never got anyone there, actually. But your Hungry Heart is on the right track. Your soul longs for God."

Genuine worship of God begins with a hungry heart! God is spirit, and those who worship him, worship him with their spirits, or with their hearts, and in truth: *in spirit*, meaning a real spiritual connection with God; and *in truth*, meaning authentic, real worship, not some kind of external hocus pocus conducted at the right place, while trying to look like the right people.

Jesus' answer to that woman still hits us on the numbers today.

7. Worship Results in Change

Finally, in both testaments, worship effects change. Worship drives all other dimensions of our walk with God in this world; when we worship, we are changed. Isaiah emerged from his encounter with God a changed man. Not only was he cleansed, his heart was changed too. He wanted to be part of God's solution rather than part of the old human problem: "Here am I. Send me!" (Isa. 6:8). And Paul assures us that as we all reflect the Lord's glory, we "are being transformed into his likeness with ever-increasing glory, which comes from the Lord" (2 Cor. 3:18).

Worship effects change.

The primary business of the church is not evangelism, as important as this mission is. The primary business is not compassionate service and justice, as God-like as these are. But the primary business of the church is worship. According to the apostle John in the book of Revelation, the central hope of a struggling church, threatened by doctrinal confusion within and persecution without, is to worship God. Worship is the fountain source from which all else flows. Worship energizes renewal and sustains us for the far journey. The sequence runs like this:

1. *Worship*—Worship sensitizes us to the nature and power of a holy, majestic, and loving God.

2. *Changed hearts*—When we genuinely draw near to God in worship, he inevitably changes our hearts.

3. *Changed character*—Changed hearts result in changed character. His nature begins to shape ours. We long for his will. His passions begin to inflame ours. We grow in our ability to discern the needs and feelings of others.

4. *Compassion, service, and justice*—God-formed character is expressed in compassion, service, and justice. Worship that does not produce these virtues is false worship.

5. *Evangelistic credibility*—Lifestyles of compassion, service, and justice underwrite the credibility of evangelistic witness.

6. *God is glorified*—Credible evangelistic witness brings people from darkness to light, from death to life, and from the power of Satan to become worshipers of the living God. Thus the cycle continues: new conversions . . . new worshipers . . . new changed hearts.

Oh, yes, the roots of worship run deep into the soil of both Old and New Testaments: The *reason* we worship is God; the *expression* of worship is in word and praise; the *experience* of worship includes feelings of awe, sorrow, joy, penitence, and jubilation; and the *results* of worship are that God is exalted, we are changed, and ministry is generated.

It's always been that way. So with the hymnist we sing:

> Oh, God, our help in ages past,
>   Our hope for years to come,
> Be Thou our guard while life shall last,
>   And our eternal home!
>
> Before the hills in order stood,
>   Or earth received her frame,
> From everlasting Thou art God,
>   To endless years the same.[4]

From the day Adam first acknowledged God at the fresh dawning of creation, through the day Abraham built roadside altars, through the temple halls ringing with psalms and shouts, through the quietness of the synagogue, through the house churches of Rome, on through catacombs, cathedrals, cabins, classrooms, and church sanctuaries, on and on through the book of Revelation where the elders fall down in a crowd of angels and worship before the throne—through endless years the same. May we all worship God according to whole Bible!

---

1. Isaac Watts, "O God, Our Help in Ages Past," *Songs of Faith and Praise*, Alton Howard, ed., (West Monroe, La.: Howard Publishing Co., 1994), 522.

2. Walter Brueggemann, *Israel's Praise: Doxology Against Idolatry and Ideology* (Philadelphia: Fortress Press), 12.

3. Summarized from Russell N. Squire, *Church Music* (St. Louis: Bethany Press, 1962).

4. Watts, 522.

MIKE COPE

◆

He Who Lives Forever

The God Who Is Worthy of Praise

CHAPTER TWO

W ho is like the Lord our God,
the One who sits enthroned on high,
who stoops down to look
on the heavens and the earth?
(Ps. 113:5–6)

In his book *The Man Who Mistook His Wife for a Hat*, neurologist Oliver Sacks describes a "lost mariner" who was admitted to their Home for the Aged near New York City in 1975 with a transfer note reading, "Helpless, demented, confused, and disoriented." The note seemed inappropriate at first since Jimmie G., as Sacks calls him, seemed like a normal, cheerful, handsome forty-nine year old.

As Dr. Sacks walked into the room for their first meeting, Jimmie G. met him with a warm, exuberant greeting. He talked about his upbringing in Connecticut, about his days in school, and about his experience in the navy in the mid-forties. The strange part of the conversation was that when he began talking about his navy days, he switched to present tense. He spoke as if it were still 1945 and he were still nineteen.

The neurologist left the room for a couple minutes and then returned. Jimmie G. again met him warmly, introducing himself as if they'd never met. This was a man with perfect memory up to 1945; but amnesia had wiped out everything since then. He had no recent-memory ability.

As conversations continued over the next months, Dr. Sacks kept hearing about Jimmie G.'s brother who was in accounting school and who was engaged to "some girl from Oregon." Later he found out that this brother and this woman were married and that he'd been an accountant for thirty years. He learned that Jimmie was a whiz at checkers but that he couldn't play chess. The movements were too slow, so he couldn't remember what had happened earlier in the game.

Sacks couldn't help wondering eventually if this "lost mariner" was still a full person. "Is this man's essence gone?" he asked. "Does he even have a soul?" When he asked Jimmie G.'s spiritual advisers, they told him to "watch Jimmie in chapel and judge for yourself."

> I did, and I was moved, profoundly moved and impressed, because I saw here an intensity and steadiness of attention and concentration that I had never seen before in him or conceived him capable of. . . . Fully, intensely, quietly, in the quietude of absolute concentration and attention, he entered and partook of the Holy Communion. He was wholly held, absorbed, by a feeling. There was no forgetting, no Korsakoff's [Syndrome] then, nor did it seem possible or imaginable that there should be; for he was no longer at the mercy of a faulty and fallible mechanism—that of meaningless sequences and memory traces—but was absorbed in an act, an act of his whole being, which carried feeling and meaning in an organic continuity and unity, a continuity and unity so seamless it could not permit any break.
>
> Clearly Jimmie found himself, found continuity and reality, in the absoluteness of spiritual attention and act.[1]

In your mind, watch the video for a moment. Watch this disoriented man with Korsakoff's Syndrome walk into the chapel to worship. Picture the confused lines on his face disappear for a moment as he remembers briefly in worship who he is. And that is the heart of worship: that we remember who we are by remembering that God is the ultimate reality, the one who created us and recreated us in Jesus Christ. In worship we recall that he has chosen us as sons and daughters, having reconciled us through the death and resurrection of his Son. And there we are stirred to remember that we are part of a people, a community of believers.

The first commandment warns us to have no other gods before the Lord God. How easy it is for us to believe that we can find life in something or someone other than God. We sometimes expect to find it in our spouses, our children, our jobs. But they can't give us life. In worship, we remember who it is that can!

In worship we remember who we are by remembering that God is the ultimate reality.

People who aren't filled with God's Spirit can never really understand what worship is about. In Stephen Carter's *The Culture of Disbelief,* he tells of hearing a teaser for a story on network news. Just before taking a break, they asked the question, "When is a church more than just a place of worship?" Do you hear the implications of "just"?

Christians believe that the church is primarily a place of worship. Worship is the first and primary business of God's people. All other acts of the church grow out of this one.

Worship is a *counterfeit detector.* It exposes the competing, conflicting worldviews that are passed off as reality. In worship, the community of faith reminds itself of the alternative world that God has ordered.[2]

Worship is also an *alignment center.* We pull into the station with our wheels heading the wrong way—worshiping our careers, our money, our friends—and there remember that Jesus is the only Way and Truth and Life.

And worship is a *compass recalibrator*. It tells us again which way is "due north." At times we've heard people pray at the end of an assembly, "Bless us now as we go out into the real world." But I believe that worship is the closest we ever come to the real world. Our eyes have been opened in the gospel to see the unseen!

Worship as Entertainment

Worship, at its best, is a performance or entertainment. But we must remember who the audience is. Soren Kierkegaard said worship has three components: the performers, the prompter, and the audience. It is vital to know who plays each part!

The whole congregation makes up the performers. Each one consciously and whole-heartedly acknowledges that God is God, that he is the mighty Creator and Redeemer who is worthy of our full devotion. The worship leader is the prompter. This is the person, who in addition to performing, leads the other performers (in song, prayer, and Scripture).

But here's the key: God is the audience! We don't worship primarily to be taught by a preacher or to be pleased with the music or to be fed by the fellowship or to reach the unbeliever; we worship to encounter God and to praise him. "Praise," as Walter Brueggemann has aptly said, "is the duty and delight, the ultimate vocation of the human community; indeed, of all creation."[3] Or as the psalmist declares, "To him belongs eternal praise" (Ps. 111:10).

There is a great cultural tug here, because in most arenas we are the audience: athletic teams play to us, politicians appeal to us, actors and actresses perform for us. But in worship, we are not the audience. Worship isn't an Olympic event whose performance we are asked to rate; nor is it a giant, psychiatric couch where our wants are explored or a monstrous, corporate pep rally where excitement is stirred. It is a performance at the throne room of God with him in the center.

The response of a friend of mine to this picture of worship is quite insightful:

> Your [Kierkegaard's] "symphonic" metaphor for worship profoundly affected me this morning. I suppose it harkens back to my training as a musician.
>
> If, in fact, God is the audience for our "performance," there might be some challenging implications. As a musician, I have been involved in some performances that exalted me to feelings of artistic consummation, and also in some that I knew were not up to a rigorous musical standard, but in both cases, I participated anyway. As I did, I tried to make my own contribution to the performance the best it could be. I was trying to focus on the impression that might be made on the audience, rather than on my own reaction to how the effort might fall short. It is true that in the good performances this was easier than in the bad, but the same process is called for by a conscientious musician in either situation. The audience's needs should take a higher priority than the player's, and the show must go on.
>
> If corporate worship is a performance for God that involves the entire body of worshipers, shouldn't we be willing and conscientious performers, regardless of our own impressions of the quality of the presentation? . . . How does God feel

when I make value judgments about corporate worship experiences that don't fit my personal aesthetic? I don't think this means I am to be nondiscerning about whether what is done and said conforms to God's will as revealed in his word. I do think it means that I ought to be careful about refusing to pitch in with the general effort. Such an action might place me in the position of being judged as a poor performer by the very audience I ought, above all others, to be trying to please.

We should not, I think, base our evaluation of the experience only on the impression it makes on us. We should rather remember that only God's evaluation counts, and that only he can hear and see the performance in the entire spiritual context in which it exists.

Our place in this performance is spotlighted by the focus on "bowing down" before God in worship. In both Hebrew and Greek, primary words for worship described God's people bowing before him. This prostration shows that he is high and holy, worthy of our full allegiance. Because we are wired differently, we have different preferences of how this "bowing down" in worship takes place, but we still must all offer God our deepest praise.

An editor of the book of Psalms has placed doxologies at the end of the five sections of psalms that call us to this praise:

Praise be to the Lord, the God of Israel,
from everlasting to everlasting.
Amen and Amen.
(Ps. 41:13)

Praise be to the Lord God, the God of Israel,
  who alone does marvelous deeds.
Praise be to his glorious name forever;
  may the whole earth be filled with his glory.
    Amen and Amen.
                              (Ps. 72:18–19)

Praise be to the Lord forever!
  Amen and Amen.
                              (Ps. 89:52)

Praise be to the Lord, the God of Israel,
  from everlasting to everlasting.
Let all the people say, "Amen!"
Praise the Lord!
                              (Ps. 106:48)

Praise the Lord.
Praise God in his sanctuary;
  praise him in his mighty heavens.
Praise him for his acts of power;
  praise him for his surpassing greatness.
Praise him with the sounding of the trumpet,
  praise him with the harp and lyre,
praise him with tambourine and dancing,
  praise him with the strings and flute,
praise him with the clash of cymbals,
  praise him with resounding cymbals.
Let everything that has breath praise the Lord.
Praise the Lord.
                              (Ps. 150)

These doxologies remind us that "from the rising of
the sun to the place where it sets, the name of the Lord
is to be praised" (Ps. 113:3). God's people are called to

proclaim "hallelujah" (praise to Yahweh) because of his creation (Ps. 104), his deliverance (Ps. 105), his patience (Ps. 106), and his eternal glory (Rev. 19:1, 3, 4, 6).

But who is this God we worship? According to Scripture, we encounter him and know him through the story of his redeeming work. God doesn't hand us a portfolio listing his central characteristics; rather, he reveals himself through his mighty acts. We know him through what he has done and continues to do.

The Transcendent, Holy God

Our understanding of God begins by realizing that he is not a created being. We carry the image of God, but he is not made in the image of humans. He is a wholly other, sovereign, infinite, holy, powerful, unapproachable God. In Paul's words, he is "the blessed and only Ruler, the King of kings and Lord of lords, who alone is immortal and who lives in unapproachable light, whom no one has seen or can see" (1 Tim. 6:15–16).

We can't even begin to grasp his majesty. We are surely like slugs trying to contemplate a human being. We can only begin to capture a few faint notions of his power and holiness. Those who glimpsed his glory in Scripture were dumbstruck and terrified:

- Israel huddled in fear and trembled as Moses alone was allowed to set foot on Sinai.

- Job, after hearing from the Lord, cried: "I am unworthy—how can I reply to you? . . . My ears had heard of you but now my eyes have seen you. Therefore I despise myself and repent in dust and ashes." (Job 40:4; 42:5, 6)

- Habakkuk, after entering the watchtower and waiting for God's answer, was seized by dread: "I heard and my heart pounded, my lips quivered at the sound; decay crept into my bones, and my legs trembled." (Hab. 3:16)

- Peter, recognizing the glory of God in the works of Jesus, responded: "Go away from me, Lord; I am a sinful man!" (Luke 5:8)

- John, having received a revelation of Christ's glory, "fell at his feet as though dead." (Rev. 1:17)[4]

The "Song of Moses" in the Old Testament and the "Song of Moses and the Lamb" in the New Testament recognize so clearly that our God is unique in his glory:

> Who among the gods is like you, O Lord?
>   Who is like you—
>   majestic in holiness,
>   awesome in glory,
>   working wonders?
>   (Exod. 15:11)

> Great and marvelous are your deeds,
>   Lord God Almighty.
> Just and true are your ways,
>   King of the ages.
> Who will not fear you, O Lord,
>   and bring glory to your name?
> For you alone are holy.
> All nations will come
>   and worship before you,
> for your righteous acts have been revealed.
>   (Rev. 15:3–4)

"Praise and glory and wisdom and thanks and honor and power and strength" are given to him (Rev. 7:12) because he deserves a whole life response.

God's Infinite Holiness

God's transcendent nature is seen in his infinite holiness. "Holy and awesome is his name," declares one biblical author (Ps. 111:9). In one sense, the word "holy" tells us that God is separate and unique. We can be God-like, but we cannot be God. "I am God, and not man— the Holy One among you," God reminds us (Hos. 11:9b). In our personality, we are more like God than we are like a cricket; but in our finiteness, we are more like a cricket than like God. As German theologian Rudolf Otto wrote, holiness in this sense refers to an "awful mystery" which we are both drawn to and repelled by. We desire both to run to the God of love and to draw back in reverent fear.

In a related sense, the word "holy" notifies us that God is wholly pure. In him there is no hint of impurity. Sin separates us from God because God is unadulterated light (Isa. 59:2).

In the vision Isaiah had, heavenly seraphs were calling out to each other:

> Holy, holy, holy is the Lord Almighty;
>   the whole earth is full of his glory.
>   (Isa. 6:3)

The threefold expression—holy, holy, holy—is a Hebrew way of expressing the concept of "holiest." There is no one to whom God can be compared.

Immediately Isaiah felt he was ruined. "Woe to me!" he cried. The lack of confession and godly sorrow in the Christian community likely stems from our failure to focus on the absolute holiness of God. When we compare ourselves to other people, we notice that we aren't all that bad. But when we measure ourselves next to God, we can only ask for mercy. Only when a coal was taken from the altar and used to purge Isaiah's lips was he able to stand in God's presence and respond to his call.

God's Infinite Power

God's transcendence also points us to his infinite power. All nations, kings, and armies pale before him. He is able to do "immeasurably more than all we ask or imagine" (Eph. 3:20).

The lack of confession and godly sorrow in the Christian community likely stems from our failure to focus on the absolute holiness of God.

Several times the Old Testament underscores the Lord's power by showing how emaciated other gods look next to his robust being. Whether the gods are those of Egypt (Exod. 1–12) or Philistia (1 Sam. 5:1–5) or Canaan (1 Kings 18), they are nothing compared to the God of Abraham, Isaac, and Jacob. All people have to admit when seeing his power, "The Lord—he is God! The Lord—he is God!" (1 Kings 18:39). Deliverance can only come to Israel because his "right hand . . . was majestic in power" (Exod. 15:6). And deliverance only comes to God's people today because in his great might he "disarmed the powers and authorities, he made a public spectacle of them, triumphing over them by the cross" (Col. 2:15).

Several years ago, when Stacy King was a rookie player with the Chicago Bulls, he made a brief appearance in a game in which Michael Jordan scored sixty-nine points. After the game, when all the players were asked to give their reflections, King said, "I'll always remember it as the evening Michael Jordan and I combined for 70 points." The people of God always remember that what they have become is possible not because of their strength and creativity but because of the unimaginable power of their God.

God's Infinite Wisdom

In addition to God's infinite holiness and power, the transcendence of God directs us to his infinite wisdom.

> Who has understood the mind of the Lord,
> or instructed him as his counselor?
> Whom did the Lord consult to enlighten him,
> and who taught him the right way?
> Who was it that taught him knowledge
> or showed him the path of understanding? . . .
> His understanding no one can fathom.
> (Isa. 40:13–14, 28)

Paul reaches back to this declaration of God's infinite wisdom when he bursts into praise:

> Oh, the depth of the riches of the wisdom and
> knowledge of God!
> How unsearchable his judgments,
> and his paths beyond tracing out!
> "Who has known the mind of the Lord?
> Or who has been his counselor?"
> "Who has ever given to God,
> that God should repay him?"

For from him and through him and to him are all
things.
To him be the glory forever! Amen.
(Rom. 11:33–36)

After all our attempts to explain the "whys" of God's
creation and redemption ("Why is there suffering?"
"Why have we been chosen?"), we have to admit that
God's ways are higher than our ways (Isa. 55:8–9). We
have only been allowed to glimpse his understanding
through his Spirit's revelation. He is sovereign in his
wise decisions and answers to no one.

As churches today are experiencing revival in worship, we must remember that the ultimate revival experience is to live in the presence of this God who is far
above our most diligent efforts. David Wells has cap-
tured so well our need to return to God:

> It is this God, majestic and holy in his being, this
> God whose love knows no bounds because his ho-
> liness knows no limits, who has disappeared from
> the modern evangelical world. He has been re-
> placed in many quarters by a God who is slick and
> slack, whose moral purposes turn out to be avun-
> cular advice that we can disregard or negotiate as
> we see fit, whose Word is a plaything for those
> who wish merely to listen to themselves, whose
> Church is a mall in which the religious, their pock-
> ets filled with the coin of need, do their business.
> We seek happiness, not righteousness. We want to
> be fulfilled, not filled. We are interested in satis-
> faction, not a holy dissatisfaction with all that is
> wrong. . . . If the Church can begin to find a place
> for theology by refocusing itself on the centrality
> of God, if it can rest upon his sufficiency, if it can

recover its moral fiber, then it will have something to say to a world now drowning in modernity.[5]

In worship, we can begin to remember again who we are by looking first at this God who made the world.

> Ascribe to the Lord, O families of nations,
> ascribe to the Lord glory and strength.
> Ascribe to the Lord the glory due his name;
> bring an offering and come into his courts.
> Worship the Lord in the splendor of his holiness;
> tremble before him, all the earth.
> (Ps. 96:7–9)

The Immanent, Loving God

When Psalm 113 tells us that God sits enthroned on high, it presents the great truth of God's otherness; no one can compare to him. But then the psalm whispers that this same God "stoops down to look on the heavens and the earth." Why would he do this? Why would he bother to look? As one biblical writer asked, What are human beings that you are mindful of them, mortals that you care for them? (Ps. 8:4).

The reason God "stoops down to look" at us is that he is not just a holy God, he is also a loving God who has chosen again and again to draw near to us. Out of love, he called forth the first humans to live in his garden. When they proved unfaithful to him, he continued to be faithful to them. He called a man, Abraham, and through him a nation, Israel, to be his covenant people. He bathed these men and women in love, but they continually rejected him. Even then he loved them enough to punish them, seeking to turn their hearts toward salvation. Finally, having sent prophet after prophet to declare his loving intentions, God came himself in Jesus Christ. In this sacrificial gift, we meet the full extent of God's love: "This is love: not that we loved God, but that he loved us and sent his Son as an atoning sacrifice for our sins" (1 John 4:10).

The very Scriptures that declare God's distance also proclaim his nearness. Though God is "majestic in holiness, awesome in glory, working wonders," he still is a God of unfailing love who leads his people to redeem them (Exod. 15:11, 13). Though the heavens cannot contain him, still he chooses in grace to dwell among us (1 Kings 8:23–27). Even though he lives "in a high and holy place," he mercifully descends to enliven the spirit of those who are contrite and lowly (Isa. 57:15).

Powerful word pictures seek to convince us of the desperate love of this covenant God. He is a father who longs for his sons and daughters (Hos. 11). He is like a mother who could never forget her children (Isa. 49). He is a husband who longs for the faithfulness of his wife (Ezek. 16). He is a shepherd who "gathers the lambs in his arms and carries them close to his heart" (Isa. 40:11).

Throughout Scripture we meet a God who cannot be trusted to leave people alone in their sin! Out of unfathomable love, he pursues us over and over. He is a personal, merciful, approachable Father who is attentive to us in a way that he surely doesn't have to be! He is an Eternal Lover who even sent his Son to live among people, to die on their behalf, and to be raised for them.

This is the amazing God whom we gather to worship. He is a God who deserves our full hearts of praise because he is both absolutely holy and absolutely loving.

Praise Yahweh, everybody!
Applaud Yahweh, all people!
His love has taken over our lives;
Yahweh's faithful ways are eternal.
    Hallelujah!

(Ps. 117 THE MESSAGE)

Implications for Our Worship

How do we worship a transcendent-but-immanent, holy-yet-loving God? Following are a few modest suggestions.

Direct Our Worship to God

Let us remember to direct our worship to God. It is entirely appropriate to sing to each other about God, about his word, and about heaven. There is certainly an important place for encouragement, fellowship, and teaching in our assemblies, but let's not forget that we gather primarily to praise God! We become lost, in Charles Wesley's words, in "wonder, love, and praise."[6] A "call to worship" from Scripture at the beginning of our assemblies can be a helpful way to remind us to "come before him with thanksgiving and extol him with music and song" (Ps. 95:2). This scriptural invitation to worship helps us remember that the whole universe continually praises the Lord without ceasing (see, e.g., Ps. 98:7–9) and that it is our turn to join in with the ethereal choir.

Let's be generous in our appropriation of songs that applaud the Lord for his gracious deeds; let's take plenty of time to pray; let's have time to sense his presence among us. It might help to remember that each gathering is a performance with God as the audience. The ultimate test is this: Was he pleased with our sacrifice of praise?

Emphasize Participation by All

Let us emphasize participation by the whole congregation. Since all Christians, rather than just a few individuals, are the performers, we should seek to provide as much active participation as possible. The practice of weekly communion allows the whole church to proclaim the Lord's death until he comes (1 Cor. 11:26). While there is a place for hearing one person or a group of people share a song, prayer, or Scripture while others worship quietly (but still actively!), our greater emphasis should likely be on songs, prayers, and Scriptures that can be sung and read together by all people.

We must not lose sight of the fact that it is God's favor we seek. We are performing for him, not for people!

Haven't many subconsciously imagined themselves the audience of our assemblies? Some, raised on schooling models of church, seem to slip into autopilot until we get to the "central event"—the sermon. They coast through communion and prayers, patiently awaiting the lesson.

Some don't sing when they don't like the songs (because they're too old, too new, too fast, too slow). But are we the audience? Some don't give when they don't like what's happening at their congregation. But are we the audience? Some spend Sunday afternoon evaluating what happened in worship. But are we the audience?

Worship planners are wise who remember the different preferences of the congregation. Because we have many people who like traditional songs, we sing lots of old, faithful hymns. And because we have many who like newer songs, we also sing lots of songs that require words to be printed in our bulletin or displayed on a screen. Since the whole congregation is performing to God, it seems appropriate to include aspects of worship for people in their "native tongue." But as we seek this variety, we must not lose sight of the fact that it is God's favor we seek. We are performing for him, not for people!

Remember How Dependent We Are

Let us in worship remember how dependent we are on God. No other person can fill our deepest needs. And we certainly can't fill our own deepest longings!

Much preaching and writing about the misuse of money and sex seems to miss the point. Beneath materialism and sexual immorality is a deeper sin: we have broken the first commandment. We have tried, in a myriad of ways, to find true life apart from the holy, loving God. Any time we seek fulfillment apart from him, we are doomed to frustration and failure.

Popular books on marriage seek to solve marital conflict by getting husbands and wives to meet the needs of their spouses. While it is surely true that we must serve one another out of love, we would be better off telling Christian husbands and wives that they can never have their deepest needs filled by another person. Any time we think we can, we set ourselves up for disappointment. Only God can care for us!

In worship, let us confess our absolute dependence on him. Let us confess that we aren't powerful enough, smart enough, or resourceful enough to guide our own lives. Worship is a regular declaration of dependence.

Learn to Enjoy God

Let us learn in worship to enjoy God. Let us learn to explode with joy like Isaiah: "I delight greatly in the Lord; my soul rejoices in my God" (Isa. 61:10). God seeks a loving relationship with us. In that relationship—and there alone—can we find true happiness.

John Ortberg has written that high-powered television ads have made his children believe that their little souls have a McDonald's-shaped vacuum: "Our hearts are restless till they find their rest in a Happy Meal," they seem to believe.

But we know, don't we, that Augustine was right in his Confessions? Our souls are restless until they rest in God! In worship we come as starving refugees, needing to be fed. And we are fed, not by memorizing information about God, but by enjoying the feast of God himself.

> We taste Thee, O Thou Living Bread,
> And long to feast upon Thee still:
> We drink of Thee, the Fountainhead
> And thirst our souls from Thee to fill.
> —Bernard of Clairvaux

1. Oliver Sacks, *The Man Who Mistook His Wife for a Hat*, (New York: Summit Books, 1985), 36.

2. See Walter Brueggemann, *Israel's Praise: Doxology Against Idolatry and Ideology* (Minneapolis: Fortress Press, 1989).

3. Ibid., 1.

4. See Mike Cope, *One Holy Hunger* (Fort Worth: Sweet Publishing, 1993), 72 ff.

5. David Wells, *No Place for Truth* (Grand Rapids, Mich.: William B. Eerdmans Publishing Co., 1993), 300–301.

6. "Love Divine," *Songs of Faith and Praise* (West Monroe, La.: Howard Publishing Co.), 140.

RANDALL J. HARRIS

◆

A People of Unclean Lips

Humans in Worship

"**B**uilding churches on biblical theology is not a way that has been tried and found wanting. For the most part, it has not yet been tried." I could not agree more with this observation of Tom Olbricht, chairman of the Religion Division at Pepperdine University, as it applies to church life generally and our topic of worship more particularly. Whether we are going to have renewal in worship is not the question: worship forms are bound to change. (Have you noticed you almost never hear a good Gregorian chant in our congregations?) The real question is whether new forms will be grounded in solid biblical theology or will answer to nothing more substantive than changing whims of taste and style.

If we are committed to allowing Scripture to lead us along the path of deeper worship, an understanding of the scriptural view of human nature is essential. The most influential work in theology for the last five hundred years, John Calvin's *Institutes of the Christian Religion,* begins with this simple observation: "Our wisdom . . . consists almost entirely of two parts: the knowledge of God and of ourselves." As crucial as the knowledge of God is to any theology of worship, our picture is not complete until we understand the human dilemma.

Our first task here is to answer the question, "Who are we?" and then to show how answering this question sheds light on the experience of worship. It is no accident that upon seeing the magnificence of God, Isaiah responds,

> Woe to me! I am ruined! For I am a man of unclean lips, and I live among a people of unclean lips, and my eyes have seen the King, the Lord Almighty. (6:5)

Understanding the appropriateness of this response is the key to our discussion.

Defining Who We Are

Human Attempts to Understand Man

The biblical view of human beings has not been without competitors. Philosophers, psychologists, and sociologists throughout the centuries have offered their solutions to the riddle of human existence. Plato and Aristotle set the direction for the western intellectual tradition by emphasizing the unique rational abilities of human beings. They were convinced that life lived according to reason would lead to the good life, and so emphasis was placed on developing intellectual capacities. Yet, the last 2,000 years have suggested that the wisdom of the Greeks is folly. Despite unprecedented strides in education, science, and the life of the mind, answers to our most fundamental problems still elude us.

Modern psychologists like Freud and Skinner have looked for answers in quite different directions. Behaviorist B. F. Skinner was convinced that human beings are like all other animals in how they learn. They simply respond to stimuli in perfectly predictable ways. Human beings are not endowed with either freedom or dignity. Like Pavlov's dogs, who salivate when they hear a bell, humans mechanistically respond in accordance with their programming. Therefore, if you want a better human being, you simply must do a better job of programming. So the key to the good life is not anything internal to the person but a matter of controlling outside stimuli. But despite our efforts to improve the environment around us, all the miseries of being human persist.

Freud, on the other hand, suggested that the problem was found more with our internal processing of events. We need not pursue the details of Freud's sometimes bizarre, often insightful theories at this point. But I would simply observe that after using the therapeutic model to deal with our internal conflicts for a couple of generations, we hardly appear to be healthier as individuals or as a society.

And as the Marxist dream has come crashing down all over the world in our time, it is almost passé to discuss Marx's views that the human dilemma can only be understood in political, material, and economic terms. After politics and economics have offered their best, the human struggle continues unabated.

In our age, when the notion of personal responsibility seems to have disappeared, we are tempted to run to the theories of existentialist philosopher Jean Paul/ Sartre who insists that we are responsible for every aspect of our lives (even our emotions) and that the good life is found in taking responsibility for our decisions. But for many of us, it is precisely the inability to take and maintain control of life that is the problem. How do we become lord of our own life? Can Scripture help us in ways these theories have not?

The Biblical View of Man

What of the biblical view? Even a cursory observation of the Bible's worship book, Psalms, suggests a unique and profound understanding of the human condition. Note the following passages, which declare opposite conclusions about the nature of human beings.

When I consider your heavens,
>   the work of your fingers,
the moon and the stars,
>   which you have set in place,
what is man that you are mindful of him,
>   the son of man that you care for him?
You made him a little lower than the
>   heavenly beings
>   and crowned him with glory and honor.
You made him ruler over the works of your hands;
>   you put everything under his feet:
all flocks and herds,
>   and the beasts of the field,
the birds of the air,
>   and the fish of the sea,
>   all that swim the paths of the seas.
>   (Ps. 8:3–8)

As for man, his days are like grass,
>   he flourishes like a flower of the field;
the wind blows over it and it is gone,
>   and its place remembers it no more.
>   (Ps. 103:15–16)

The Dual Nature of Man

To understand this apparent contradiction—that man is both lord of the earth crowned with glory *and* like a flower that fades and dies in a day without even leaving a memory—is to gain great insight into the experience of being human and into the experience of worship.

From the very beginning of Scripture, this dual nature is declared. In Genesis 2:7, God breathed into man's nostrils the breath of life, and he became a "living being"—just like the land and sea animals (1:20, 24). Human beings are creatures: they are created. They share the basic limitations of every other animal in the created order, which we might term "finiteness." As humans, we are subject to basic biological needs, given to certain instinctual drives, limited by our embodiment (I have been deprived of the thrill of dunking a basketball), and subject to death. (One should note that Adam and Eve were not immortal by nature. It was by virtue of access to the tree of life that they continued life. Loss of that access led to certain death.)

But, of course, this is only half the story. For there is also something else said about human beings that makes them totally unique within God's creation.

> Then God said, "Let us make man in our image, in our likeness, and let them rule over the fish of the sea and the birds of the air, over the livestock, over all the earth, and over all the creatures that move along the ground." So God created man in his own image, in the image of God he created him; male and female he created them. (Gen. 1:26–27)

Despite all they share with other animals, humans are set apart by virtue of being made in the image of God. What does this mean?

The text does not explicitly tell us, but the image of God is linked with the task of ruling the earth. I am inclined to believe that God's image in us is the totality of characteristics that allow us to perform this function. This would include such things as rationality, self-reflection, freedom, creativity, and social and linguistic abilities. All these things taken together, which allow us to exercise an almost god-like prerogative on the earth, constitute the image of God.

So now we see that our apparently contradictory psalms are not contradictory at all, but in fact indicate the truth about how God made us. We are both finite and creaturely on the one hand, and transcendent by virtue of the image of God within us on the other. No view of human nature is correct that misses either dimension.

Imbalance Leads to a Distorted View

What kind of distortions of our true nature do we get if we emphasize one aspect to the neglect of the other? Suppose we see only the creaturely aspects of human beings? What we come out with looks very much like B. F. Skinner's behaviorism. We are simply slobbering dogs, to be manipulated by ringing bells. If, on the other hand, we emphasize only the human's highest capacities and forget his creatureliness, we get the ugliest sort of humanism that sees us as gods and breeds a dangerous overconfidence in our ability to successfully control all things and bring about a utopian society.

The human being's unique position does create a dilemma, as the story of the fall indicates. The tempter's snare is depicted thus: "'You will not surely die,' the serpent said to the woman. 'For God knows that when you eat of it your eyes will be opened, and you will be like God, knowing good and evil'" (Gen. 3:4–5).

Anxiety Is Unique to Man

The question this raises is, What is there about the human situation that leads Adam and Eve to succumb to this offer? Having been given so much by God, why do they wager it all on this devil's bet? I think Reunhold

Niebuhr has pointed us to the right solution with the concept of *anxiety*.[1] Only the creature on the boundary, the human, is plagued with anxiety. The combination that leads to anxiety is finiteness plus a self-reflective *awareness* of one's finiteness.

Neither animals, who die but do not worry over it, nor God, who cannot die, are beset by anxiety. Human beings, however, who not only die but are able to reflect on their own mortality, are subject to the insecurity that produces anxiety. We must find a way to face our own demise.

Anxiety Leads to Sensuality

If I could only become an animal without awareness of my impending doom, how happy life could be! I could simply live life gratifying every desire of my body, and then one day—without a worried thought—I would simply drop dead (or perhaps get run over by a bus). In fact, many attempt to live life in this very way. This leads to what are often called the sins of sensuality. I live as fast and furiously as possible in order to avoid those quiet moments when the nagging anxiety caused by the sureness of the grave creeps in. But despite my best efforts to become just a beast, this is not my true nature, and the truth I cannot face stalks me. I am not just an animal.

Anxiety Leads to Idolatry

But there is another solution to my anxiety. If I cannot succeed in becoming an animal, thus denying death, perhaps I can become like God. This, of course, is the path taken by the original sinners. What this implies is that I will become the source of my own security. This leads to the various sins of pride and points us to the most fundamental human problem: *idolatry.* Since we moderns are much too sophisticated to fall for the crass idolatry described in the Old Testament, is this really such a problem? As Habakkuk says,

> Of what value is an idol, since a man has carved it?
>   Or an image that teaches lies?
> For he who makes it trusts in his own creation;
>   he makes idols that cannot speak.
> Woe to him who says to wood, "Come to life!"
>   Or to lifeless stone, "Wake up!"
> Can it give guidance?
>   It is covered with gold and silver;
>   there is no breath in it.
>   (2:18–19)

Yet I am convinced that though we have outgrown the worship of goldplated, wood statues, idolatry is all around us and is the single greatest detriment to our worship. We may plead "not guilty" to Habakkuk's charge, but the kind of idolatry Jeremiah talks about is quite another matter.

> This is what the Lord says:
> "Let not the wise man boast of his wisdom
>   or the strong man boast of his strength
>   or the rich man boast of his riches,
> but let him who boasts boast about this:
>   that he understands and knows me,
>   that I am the Lord who exercises kindness,
>   justice and righteousness on earth,
>   for in these I delight,"
>   declares the Lord.
>   (9:23–24)

Here we are presented with three great idolatries— wisdom, power, and riches. In pursuit of these, we desperately look for a way to take control of our lives and become the source of our own security. If we just get smart enough, we will learn to control our world so that nothing bad will happen to us. If we just get enough power, no one will dare attack us and we will be safe. If we just pile up enough money, our futures will be secure. And in our anxiety, we take the same path as the original pair: we seek to be the source of our own security.

In addition to the three great idolatries listed above, we might add one more—the idolatry of religion. Placing one's trust in God and trusting in religion are quite different things. Take, for example, Jeremiah 7:

> Do not trust in deceptive words and say, "This is the temple of the Lord, the temple of the Lord, the temple of the Lord!" . . . Will you steal and murder, commit adultery and perjury, burn incense to Baal and follow other gods you have not known, and then come and stand before me in this house, which bears my Name, and say, "We are safe"—safe to do all these detestable things? (vv. 4, 9–10)

Or, even more to our point, Amos 5:

> I hate, I despise your religious feasts;
>   I cannot stand your assemblies.
> Even though you bring me burnt
>   offerings and grain offerings,
>   I will not accept them.
> Though you bring choice fellowship offerings,
>   I will have no regard for them.
> Away with the noise of your songs!
>   I will not listen to the music of your harps.

But let justice roll on like a river,
   righteousness like a never-failing stream!
                (vv. 21–24)

In the above passages, we see that trust in God has been replaced in the first case by trust in the temple and in the second by trust in the worship ritual. There is always the danger of thinking that if we just worship God correctly we will be spiritually healthy. Although this accusation is most often leveled against traditionalists ("They think that if we just use the right forms of worship it will be acceptable to God"), those who seek change and renewal in worship are just as vulnerable: "I just can't worship in that old way." "We need more emotion in our worship." "Worship should be upbeat (uplifting) and contemporary." Such phrases suggest a not-too-subtle dependence on a particular style that is as idolatrous as the dogged commitment to the worship style of a previous generation. We ought to beware of those who suggest that changes in the liturgy or worship style will solve the spiritual problems that beset us. They may, in fact, make us feel better, but like a pain-killer, they only serve to mask the very real spiritual diseases that are the source of our pain.

Man's Need for God

Scripture does provide us a way out of our dilemma. We need not become either animal or deity. All we need do is *trust God*. While this solution is very simple, it is most assuredly not easy. To admit our inadequacy as the source of our own security and to fully rest ourselves on the gentle support of God's grace is one of life's more difficult tasks.

God has always provided a method of cleansing for sinful human beings. In the Isaiah passage with which we began, Isaiah is made clean with the live coal. Under Mosaic law, the scapegoat and the day of atonement (Lev. 16) provide the means of dealing with sin. In the New Testament, Christian baptism is said to wash away sins. But in every case, it is God's action that does the work—regardless of the vehicle used.

First John 1 provides us with one of the clearest pictures of the proper relationship of God's work and the human response.

> This is the message we have heard from him and declare to you: God is light; in him there is no darkness at all. If we claim to have fellowship with him yet walk in the darkness, we lie and do not live by the truth. But if we walk in the light, as he is in the light, we have fellowship with one another, and the blood of Jesus, his Son, purifies us from all sin.
>
> If we claim to be without sin, we deceive ourselves and the truth is not in us. If we confess our sins, he is faithful and just and will forgive us our sins and purify us from all unrighteousness. If we claim we have not sinned, we make him out to be a liar and his word has no place in our lives. (1 John 1:5–10)

Note what the above passage declares. First, since God is light, those who love God will strive to be light-walkers. It is reminiscent of the Old Testament injunction to be holy as God is holy. It reminds us, as Amos has told us, that worship is no substitute for righteous living. But despite this call to righteousness, there is the recognition (stated twice) that Christians sin. How are we to deal with the fact that sin continues to plague us despite our best efforts to walk in the light? The passage indicates that both God and humans play a part in resolving the sin problem. But what is striking is how different the two roles are!

God's task is to purify us from all sin by the blood of Jesus. He provides all we need through the work of his Son. In fact, when you look at the human contribution, it is really no contribution at all! All we do is recognize our inability to solve our problem, the recognition of which leads to confession. We come to God acknowledging that we fail, expressing sorrow, and throwing ourselves on his mercy displayed through his Son.

Both God and humans play a part in resolving the sin problem. But how different the two roles are!

It is so utterly simple (though perhaps not easy) that it is startling. We are not and cannot become mere animals. We are not and cannot become gods. We are human beings who are totally dependent on God, and who thus should live in simple trust that God can do for us what we cannot do for ourselves. This simple point, which is the theme of the whole Bible, is the key to the richest and fullest worship experience. When we come to realize that God has done for us what we cannot do for ourselves, the most natural response in the world is worship.

Implications for Worship

The purpose of our study of human nature has been to gain some insight into the experience of worship and then draw some implications for our assemblies. We now turn to this latter issue. There are three basic ideas to be emphasized.

Worship Should Embody the Totality of Human Reality

First, since the totality of human reality includes the *physical, mental, emotional,* and *spiritual,* so must our worship. The oft-quoted dichotomy of right-brain or left-brain worship misses the point. God created us with all our capacities, and the attempt to elevate any one particular aspect to the exclusion of the others is bound to create tension. In fact, to do so involves a denial of our true nature.

Those who would leave behind the rational dimension of worship have forgotten who we are and how we were created.

I do not think it is any accident that God's prescribed worship ritual has always involved *physical* substance that becomes symbolic. The grape juice and unleavened bread and water in baptism are as crassly physical as the sacrificial animals of Old Testament worship. Since we are physical, such material substances are crucial to our full participation in worship. Various worship postures (kneeling or lifting hands to God) are appropriate expressions of creatures with bodies. To try to disconnect worship from the body denies that we are the "living beings" of Genesis 1.

It is certainly no coincidence that worship is a rational enterprise with a language and content to be grasped with the *mind.* In fact, Paul insists in 1 Corinthians 12–14 that the building-up of one another is dependent on the sharing of *content*. Words are crucial in our assemblies, and what we say ought to be examined carefully. The quality of a hymn is finally determined by what it says. The quest for ecstasy (worship beyond word and content) is totally inappropriate to the assembly. It is precisely the content of the faith that binds us together. Those who would leave behind the rational dimension of worship have forgotten who we are and how we were created.

This is not to say that *emotions* have no place in worship. We have examples in Scripture where worship ranges from jubilant celebration to an almost funeral-like dirge. It was precisely the mistake of the Greeks to think humans could be understood as "rational" animals. All of this is to say what should be obvious: worship should correspond to the biblical teaching on who human beings truly are.

Needless to say, worship must also reflect who we are *spiritually*. We now turn more directly to this dimension.

Worship Should Be Confessional

Second, and to my mind most important, worship ought to be confessional. In an age of feel-good worship, it is crucial that the reality of our own unworthiness before God hover over our assemblies. Only those with a deep awareness of their sin and, consequently, God's forgiveness, can plummet the deepest reaches of worship. As David says,

> Blessed is he
> 　　whose transgressions are forgiven,
> 　　whose sins are covered.
> Blessed is the man

whose sin the Lord does not count against him
and in whose spirit is no deceit.
When I kept silent,
my bones wasted away
through my groaning all day long.
For day and night
your hand was heavy upon me;
my strength was sapped
as in the heat of summer.
Then I acknowledged my sin to you
and did not cover up my iniquity.
I said, "I will confess
my transgressions to the Lord"—
and you forgave
the guilt of my sin.
(Ps. 32:1–5)

Confession has not played a prominent role in our assemblies. Perhaps we are yet unprepared to admit the brokenness that mars all of our lives. Is it possible that jubilant worship is an attempt to avoid the stark reality of our own unworthiness before God? Until the worshipers' "righteous, well-ordered" facade is melted under the withering light of God's unapproachable holiness, worship will always be superficial. Worship begins with the confession of our sinfulness and helplessness; it is a desperate cry of perishing people. In our day of concern for self-esteem, this will never be popular, but it is theologically sound. *Pride is incompatible with worship!*

Worship Should Call Us away from Idolatry

And, third, worship should call us away from idolatry and to trust in what is really real. How unfortunate and misguided is the well-intentioned prayer that asks for God's blessing as we leave worship to go out into the "real world." Nothing could be more real than the experience of worship. This, I would suggest, means that we must never lose sight of worship's *theological* character.

Perhaps an example will help make the point clear. When Elijah met the prophets of Baal on Mount Carmel in 1 Kings 18, the land was in crisis—drought had besieged it. The immediate, pressing need of the people was rain. Yet the contest was about fire. The question that needed answering was, How long will you go on limping between two opinions? If Yahweh is God, follow him; if Baal is God, follow him. Once this question was answered, everything else fell into place.

The Basis of Worship Is Trust

People bring an almost infinite variety of needs into our assembly, no doubt many worth addressing. But if Scripture is to be believed, they all come from a common root—our inability to entrust ourselves fully to God. We limp between not two but many opinions. And despite opening myself to the accusation of leading our worship into irrelevance, I am convinced we should talk about rain less and fire more. That is, worship is not primarily about dealing with the ethical or emotional or social crises that so constantly beset us but is rather a call back to the most basic issue: Whom will you trust? Worship ought to be spiritually-centered, a call to transcendence.

What's wrong with our worship assemblies? We are ready at long last to answer this question. At its root, the problem has nothing to do with the styles of the songs or the quality of the leadership or even the restrictiveness of the worship tradition. In the immortal words of Pogo, "We have met the enemy and he is us." We cannot spend our every waking moment attempting to be the source of our own security and suddenly in the moment of worship cast ourselves fully on the Lord. Only when we realize the futility of our best efforts is the ground for worship prepared. "Woe to me! I am ruined." Worship springs from the realization that what the old song says is true. "Just as I am without one plea!" If you wish to see true worship renewal in our time, the issue to be addressed is not worship but *idolatry*. For until this is done, our restlessness will find no satisfaction in change of worship style. Augustine is right when he says to God. "Our hearts are restless and find no rest until they rest in you."

---

1. See his *Nature and Destiny of Man*, vol. 1, to which I am greatly indebted.

DR. RUBEL SHELLY

◆

Where Has All the Wonder Gone?

A Responsible Challenge to Our Traditions

Worship is a discipline reserved for those whose souls retain the capacity for wonder. One can go to the right place, say the right words, do all the right things—yet never be in awe . . . never marvel . . . never encounter God . . . *never be lost in wonder.*

After all, worship is more nearly the province of children than adults. Adults figure out the physics of rainbows; children "ooh" and "aah" over them. Adults watch the magician's hands to find out where he is hiding coins and flowers and birds; children get so caught up in the event that they squeal or applaud or shout with glee. Adults manufacture, sell, and inspect ice cream; children eat it with such passion that they get it all over their faces.

Those of us who have been Christians longer and think ourselves biblically literate leaders in the church write treatises on worship, speak at worship seminars, and flash our scholarly swords at each other; babes in Christ who realize they have been rescued from this present evil age by the sacrifice of Christ actually worship. Some of them worship in very traditional and "stuffy" churches; others glorify the Lord with contemporary praise songs and in assemblies that are anything but traditional.

It is the spirit of wonder—so often reserved for little children in our world and for newborn Christians in our churches—that all of us should desire most in worship. "Shout for joy to the Lord, all the earth. Worship the Lord with gladness; come before him with joyful songs" (Ps. 100:1–2). "I am the Lord; that is my name! I will not give my glory to another or my praise to idols" (Isa. 42:8). "A time is coming and has now come when the true worshipers will worship the Father in spirit and truth, for they are the kind of worshipers the Father seeks" (John 4:23).

Perhaps one of the reasons Jesus spoke the following words is that children have a capacity for wonder that often eludes older people: "I tell you the truth, unless you change and become like little children, you will never enter the kingdom of heaven" (Matt. 18:3).

But be honest now. Does worship fill your soul with a sense of wonder and awe before God? Is it a time of real encounter between the God who seeks and your responsive soul? Is it a time when you marvel at the majesty of a holy God who has condescended to your low estate to make you his child?

It is the spirit of wonder that we should desire most in worship.

In both private and public worship, I am relearning wonder. I am starting to feel free to laugh aloud, clap my hands, or cry. I can fall to my knees or lift my hands. I can smile at my brothers or embrace strangers. These are natural experiences for children but difficult for adults.

The single most important thing that has allowed me to enter more deeply into the spirit of worship has been an emerging ability to distinguish biblical truth from church culture. Or, to say it another way, my desire for and experience of true worship has been enhanced by stretching beyond the narrow boundaries of tradition and into the broader range of biblically authorized and culturally appropriate expressions of worship.

In this presentation, I will attempt to make a passionate and biblical case for true worship. I will argue that we must submit our subjective tastes and desires to the judgment of the Word of God; I will also argue that we must learn to honor the freedom and creativity authorized by Scripture and made possible by the presence of the Holy Spirit among his people. While repeatedly insisting on the right of the Word of God to govern our worship, I will also urge that we must reject the rigid judgments of peers who would deny legitimate freedom and bind us by their compunctions.

A Top-Ten List for Preserving the Status Quo

With apologies to David Letterman, my own research staff has compiled a list of ten reasons for maintaining the status quo with regard to worship.

10. There is nothing we can improve in our worship experiences.

9. There is nothing to repent of in our history as a worshiping community.

8. We have neither calling nor obligation to make our worship more relevant to a modern world.

7. It is impossible to be both biblical and pertinent in the same worship setting.

6. The only way to worship God acceptably is to worship him in the ways we remember from childhood.

5. The worship experiences we have known in our history are fully appropriate to what a holy and perfect God deserves.

4. Our worship communicates effectively with and assists powerfully in evangelizing the lost.

3. Our public and private worship appears to captivate, inspire, and stimulate Christians to ever greater faith, love, and unity.

2. No one in our fellowship has ever expressed interest in or need for change in our worship practices.

1. We know—both intellectually and experientially —all there is to know about the worship of God.

These proffered reasons for refusing to study, change, and attempt to improve the worship experience of our churches range from the arrogant (1) to the absurd (5, 2), from the unlikely (10, 9, 7, 6) to the unbiblical (8), from the patently false (3) to the perversely fraudulent (4).

Some Preliminary Reflections on Worship

Worship, whether private or public, is neither a place nor an act (or series of acts) but *an attitude that accompanies certain actions that are authorized by and appropriate to God.* The authorized and appropriate actions are prophecy, prayer, and praise. The attitude is adoration, reverence, humility, and submission to God—summed up for us in the single word *wonder.*

Prophecy

People who come to our assemblies are not only bored but harmed by sermons that don't live where they live; they are not led to evaluate their real-life struggles in light of a relevant message from God. They

neither need nor want academic and abstract discourses
on biblical texts. They want someone to explain the
Word of God to them in simple, direct terms. Solid,
competent Bible teaching that communicates with people of the twenty-first century may sound more like sto-
rytelling than a university lecture. Check the Gospels
again, and you will find that Jesus' preaching was of
that very sort. Prophecy is a word from God that speaks
to the time and place of the hearers. Are we not remov-
ing this vital element from worship when we are lazy,
out of touch, and wearisome with our preaching?

Prayer

Although we tend to say more about preaching and
music than prayer, I am not so sure that our insuffi-
ciency in prayer isn't at the root of all our failures in
worship. Singing and Bible study
ought to have encounter with God as
their goals, but prayer *is* encounter
with God. Maybe we do not experience
the fullness of God in worship because
we do not want him there and make
the choice to exclude him. I believe we
make a choice to exclude God when we
pray shallow, rote, and trivial prayers.

*Singing and
Bible study
ought to
have
encounter
with God as
their goals,
but prayer
is encounter
with God.*

Someone who "leads" prayer in a
corporate worship context has at least
as serious a task as the one who "leads"
its Bible study. The former is typically
done extemporaneously and without
careful preparation; we would not tol-
erate that for many Sundays from a
preacher/teacher. Spiritual power in
the lives of Daniel, Jesus, and Paul was

rooted in earnest prayer; perhaps the weakness in personal faith and corporate worship we so often lament traces to carelessness about prayer.

Praise

Then there is the matter of praise. Nothing so nearly identifies a body of people as worshipers as their ability to celebrate God: insights into the Word of God and earnestness in prayer burst forth as praise, and God is cheered and applauded in culturally appropriate ways. Lost in wonder before him, the people break forth in sustained and meaningful exaltation of his presence and deeds among them.

In these critical actions of prayer, praise, and prophecy, *worship that is not relevant is not biblical.* Culturally irrelevant worship hides what is meant to be disclosed. Under a mist of tradition and culture, it obscures what is meant to be brought into view.

How We Become What We Are

The church in every generation is shaped by both biblical doctrine and cultural tradition. To a certain degree, the church's worship experience is determined by teaching that comes directly from the Word of God. To an even greater degree, however, it is bound and shaped by its evolved traditions.

It is critical for us to learn the difference between biblical doctrine and received tradition. For example, one brother recently warned against the following things in worship: hand-clapping, hand-raising, drama, eliminating invitation songs, and the use of overhead projectors.

Bless his heart! I'll bet he thinks the great issues facing the church from the unbelieving world are long hair, women wearing pants, and high school dances.

Receiving and living in the grace of God involves putting to death the evil urge of our sinful natures to dominate others. Communicating the gospel of the grace of God to a lost world means more than rearranging deck chairs on the sinking ship of our fallen culture. And worshiping within grace must have a meaning greater than debating over clapping our hands.

The Worship Principle

The Greek word most closely related to our English "worship" is *proskyneo*. The term has an interesting background.

> The basic meaning of *proskyneo*, in the opinion of most scholars, is to kiss. The prefix indicates a connection with cultic practices going back beyond Gk. history. On Egyptian reliefs worshippers are represented with outstretched hand throwing a kiss to (*pros-*) the deity. Among the Greeks the vb. is a technical term for the adoration of the gods, meaning to fall down, prostrate oneself, adore on one's knees. . . . In addition to the external act of prostrating oneself in worship, *proskyneo* can denote the corresponding inward attitude of reverence and humility.[1]

When the Jews translated the Old Testament into Greek, they translated the Hebrew word *histahawah* as *proskyneo*. *Histahawah* carries the idea of bending down, stooping, or bowing before Yahweh. Thus, by the time of the New Testament, *proskyneo* signified the bowing of oneself before God, occasionally retaining its physical sense of bending the body but always connoting the bowing of one's will to that of another. Worship, as an act of "bowing down" one's heart and life to God, meets our fundamental human needs.

Worship Gets Our Focus off Ourselves and onto God

We are caught up in our things, our situations, and our selves. True worship can never have the creature at the center; it must focus on the Creator. Even so, we worship him as an action of divine grace. He has taken the initiative to make himself known to us and to come to us in Christ, thus we move outside our narrow little worlds of self-interest to worship him in gratitude. Because he is holy and we are unholy, the encounter that takes place in worship leads to a bowing of our wills to his. *The International Standard Bible Encyclopedia* says this about worship:

> Worship, then, is the dramatic celebration of God in His supreme worth in such a manner that His "worthiness" becomes the norm and inspiration of human living. Defined in this way worship (1) places God at the center because of His worthiness; (2) avoids the tyranny of subjectivism; (3) allows for the reexamination of the self in the light of God's knowledge of us.[2]

The way to evaluate worship, then, is not by whether we "like it" or "get something out of it" but by how effective it is in drawing our attention away from ourselves and onto God.

Worship is at its best when we are least conscious of it. Like dancing or typing, we may have to go through an awkward learning period during which there is far too much self-awareness. The goal, however, is to lose self-consciousness in the event for the sake of becoming absorbed with God. Mark Horst, in an article in *Christian Century*, said,

> As soon as we come to worship looking for and expecting a worship experience, we have violated the most basic principle of this discipline. We easily become religious aesthetes capable of judging the entertainment value of a church service while remaining unaware of the reality it can open us to. Unfortunately for us, when our worship becomes self-conscious rather than God-conscious, it points not to God's reality but to its own.[3]

So, let's be sure that we really are seeking *renewal* in our worshiping lives and not merely "tinkering" with worship experiences. Some will think they have renewed worship by changing the order of events, adding a few contemporary songs, and (if radical!) using an overhead projector. These things can be helpful parts of worship renewal. They can also be mere cosmetic surgery, when what is needed is a heart transplant.

Learning to worship means learning to encounter God.

Learning to worship, then, means learning to encounter God. In that encounter experience, we see ourselves afresh and correctly before him. The vision of God in worship humbles us, moves us outside ourselves, and begins to shape us into his likeness.

Worship Brings Us into Fellowship with God's People

Worship brings us into the presence of God's people and drives away feelings of isolation and loneliness. This is why the Lord's Supper is particularly important and central to Christian worship.

Paul rebuked the Christians at Corinth for their division and isolation from one another. Among other problems in their observance of the Lord's Supper, they perpetuated their divisions into that holy service. Thus he warned them that "anyone who eats and drinks without recognizing the body of the Lord eats and drinks judgment on himself" (1 Cor. 11:29). Ralph Martin comments, "Probably we should see here an allusion to the 'body' (of 1 Cor. 10:17, looking ahead to 12:12–13), which is the church. What the Corinthians failed to discern was the unity of the Spirit that the eucharist was designed to promote and exemplify."[4]

Worship brings us into the presence of God's people and drives away feelings of isolation and loneliness.

Reflecting on Paul's censure of the Corinthians' behavior, we come to understand that the Lord's Supper in particular and worship in general are about *koinonia*. Corporate worship draws us into a community of faith—past, present, and future. While private worship is important and beneficial, it does not replace corporate worship. They serve different though complementary purposes. The former may isolate us from our brothers and sisters; the latter demands that we relate to them in the love of Christ. This has direct implications for us in that it underscores the sort of respect we should demonstrate toward each other in dealing with worship transitions and changes.

Corporate worship is an all-church experience. The notion that someone would step into the worship arena, eliminate all that is familiar and sacred to older Christians, and—in the name of reaching younger, disenfranchised, or unchurched people—trample on those people is abhorrent to me. It is equally abhorrent that older Christians would refuse and forbid more contemporary approaches to worship that we *know* can reach outsiders and nourish younger people in our fellowship.

Worship puts life issues in focus and requires us to look at all things through the eyes of God.

So what shall we do? Shall we sing "The Old Rugged Cross" and "I'll Fly Away" or "In Moments Like These" and "Thank You, Lord"? Shall we preach sermons or present drama? Shall we offer extemporaneous prayers or write them out? Shall we have a song leader or a worship team? All these questions are framed wrong. Each implies a win/lose strategy of forcing a choice between exclusive alternatives. If we operate by the principle of mutual respect, we can employ a win/win strategy by which we embrace elements from various generations, tastes, and methods of doing things.

We must not add to the sense of isolation and rivalry among human beings in the church's worship. Rather, we must learn to be inclusive. We must affirm the body in its totality. We must see that every part of the body is valuable to Christ and to us as well.

Worship Inspires a Sense of Hope

Praise lifts people out of their discouragement by bringing them into the presence of the living God. The vision of God that comes within a worship context draws worshipers to the "God center" for life. It puts life issues in focus and requires us to look at all things through the eyes of God.

Where does a discouraged soul stand to find hope? How does she learn to sing in her pain? What can convince him that sickness, loss, or betrayal can be overcome? Christ's triumph came from the unlikely scene of his gruesome death, and his experience is a promise of our own triumph. It is when the shadow of the cross falls over us again in worship that the radiance of divine reality becomes obvious. The only vantage point from which one can see life and all its issues clearly is the foot of the cross of Jesus Christ. And it is that vantage point that corporate worship maintains.

Learning from All Traditions in American Protestantism

As we understand what worship is and attempt either to lead or participate in worship that achieves the goals sketched above, it is to be expected that certain traditions will evolve.

Dan Scott, whose background is in the Pentecostal Movement, traces three streams of religious tradition that have emerged in American Protestantism. He charts them in a clear and helpful way.[5]

Worship tradition	Liturgical	Evangelical	Pentecostal
Biblical source	temple	synagogue	prophetic
Central activities	sacrament ceremony	study exposition	celebration spontaneity
Worship focus	Father	Son	Holy Spirit
Ministry model	priest	rabbi	prophet
Central concern	reverence	understanding	experience

The strengths he names in the *liturgical* tradition include such important things as continuity, connection with the past, and sensitivity to the gospel's impact on culture as well as individuals; its weaknesses are a tendency toward enslavement to the past, reverence for God to the point of alienation from him, the confusion of form with substance that can degenerate into idolatry, and a focus on social issues that neglects personal faith.

The strengths he points to in the *evangelical* tradition are such things as scholarship, commitment to orthodox doctrine, and the seeking of a personal faith commitment from people; its weaknesses can be a worship of the Bible and human intellect rather than God, poverty in worship (e.g., sometimes calling worship the "preliminaries" to preaching), a tendency toward autonomous faith that creates a weak doctrine of the church, and the neglect of social justice.

The strengths he points to in the *Pentecostal* tradition are an acute awareness of the presence of God, the expectation that God will act in contemporary life, and celebrative worship; its weaknesses he identifies as "addiction to orgiastic religious experience sometimes based on little more than experience itself" and distrust for historical Christianity.

These three "traditions" reflect, in my opinion, different personalities. Some personalities are more comfortable with intellect; others with emotion. Some gravitate toward ceremony; others toward spontaneity. As is true for individuals, churches need to seek a balance and can benefit from all three "personalities": We all need rootedness, without idolatry toward the past; we all need head involvement, without arrogance toward and a sense of personal isolation from the larger Body of Christ; and we all need heart involvement, without jettisoning the anchors of history and biblical content. Religion generally and worship in particular can be full-orbed only when all these needs are acknowledged and met.

Liturgy provides stability and continuity. Baptism and the Lord's Supper provide continuity with Christian history and are deeply rooted in the biblical text itself. The appropriate warning about liturgy is, of course, the one found repeatedly in the Old Testament prophets: the rites of faith must not be treated as ends in themselves. It is easy to go through the motions without engaging our hearts.

The evangelical head involvement keeps us firmly anchored in the Word of God. Thus we affirm Scripture to be the inspired Word of God and value its study and teaching. However, we must not judge our present-day reading of the Bible by positions taken earlier in our history. Nothing is immune to scrutiny under the searchlight of Scripture.

And the Pentecostal heart involvement engages our total beings in passionate commitment to God through Jesus Christ. Knowledge is sterile without the passion of our heart or "gut." Where the Spirit of God is present, there is life, creativity, and spontaneity.

The Problem with Tradition

Having admitted that it is perfectly normal and right to evolve worship traditions (as we certainly have!), it is sinful to elevate those traditions to a status equal with divine revelation.

Jesus had more than casual conversations with the Pharisees of his day about their evolved traditions in worship. One of the sternest of those exchanges resulted in this statement from our Lord:

> Isaiah was right when he prophesied about you hypocrites; as it is written: "These people honor me with their lips, but their hearts are far from me. They worship me in vain; their teachings are but rules taught by men." You have let go of the commands of God and are holding on to the traditions of men. (Mark 7:6–8)

Jaroslav Pelikan put it this way for moderns:

> Tradition is the living faith of the dead; traditionalism is the dead faith of the living. Tradition lives in conversation with the past, while remembering we are where and when we are and that it is we who have to decide. Traditionalism supposes that nothing should ever be done for the first time, so all that is needed to solve any problem is to arrive at the supposedly unanimous testimony of homogenized tradition.[6]

There are some critical areas in which we must act as genuine restorationists by submitting our "received views" to the careful study of Scripture. As we do so, we must realize that different people and churches will come to different personal and congregational decisions on some (if not all) of these matters.

Some Debilitating Traditions

In the following paragraphs I will challenge three areas in which we have a lot of thinking yet to do. We are heirs to culture-conditioned (i.e., nineteenth-century culture) answers to questions that must be asked again in the twentieth and twenty-first centuries. Without giving audience-driven answers that concede biblical points to the spirit of our age, it is perfectly acceptable to raise questions and to search for answers that are more biblically faithful and consistent than those to which we are heirs. We had to do that thirty years ago with regard to segregation, which both our exposition of Scripture and consistent practice had championed. Did we abandon the Bible to adopt culture? Or did we lose some cultural blinders that allowed us to see the Bible more clearly? There are other questions begging to be asked now.

Our Teaching Ministry

The first area in which I believe we must revise our understanding and practice has to do with the church's teaching ministry. In terms of corporate worship, our received tradition has us limiting the teaching of the Word of God to two methods: lecture/preaching and songs.

Since I will have more to say later about music in worship, allow me to confine this initial point to the assumption of many that lecture is the best and only means for communicating the Word of God in our corporate assemblies.

People may be more open to the study of the Bible now than at any other time within the century. The lack of Bible teaching in liberal churches has many people searching for churches that still sound a "thus saith the Lord." And many people who have been altogether unchurched in their adult lives are now casting about for a place of spiritual mooring. Sure, some of them have read Shirley MacLaine's books and have attended seminars on drum-banging in the woods, but these same people are open to the Word of God—if it is spoken to their life situation with clarity and credibility.

We must not tamper with the message, but neither can we afford to confuse the message with the method of its delivery.

I am appealing for a methodology for teaching the Bible that is faithful to the text and authoritative. Much of what the Bible says goes against the grain of our culture. It offers death as the means to life, and that by means of a torture instrument called a cross. What is right or wrong is not determined by a show of hands, but by divine revelation. Jesus still says we have to lose our lives in order to find them, and repentance is not an option but an obligation in pursuit of eternal life. But the Bible has always said these things, and they have always been countercultural. When the gospel is taught faithfully today, these themes are not omitted or "soft-peddled."

We must not tamper with the message, but neither can we afford to confuse the message with the method of its delivery. I believe there are ways other than lecture that can be used to communicate the gospel. I believe there are ways to do lecture presentations better than most of us do them. And I believe we are under obligation from God to explore and use every effective communications medium known to—and presently being developed by—humankind.

Rick Warren did some research a while back among five hundred people who were not attending church at the time. What he learned is important to all of us who care about reaching lost people with the gospel.

> Warren's survey revealed four reasons why unchurched people don't attend: (1) Sermons are boring, and irrelevant to their lives. (2) The members are unfriendly to visitors. (3) Churches seem more interested in your money than in you as a person. (4) They want quality child care if they go to church.[7]

Please note that these reasons have to do with sociology and methodology, not theology. The first reason has to do with the "boring" and "irrelevant" nature of the preaching they hear. The two terms almost surely define each other, for preaching in the most traditional style is not boring if it addresses the real-life concerns of people. Answer the questions I am asking, and it doesn't matter that you speak with a nasal whine. Speak to trivial matters that have no impact on my life, and it doesn't matter that you have the charisma of Kevin Costner.

Yet we must also come to appreciate that there are methods of communicating with people in our culture that we are not using. Sermons typically assume sequential thought patterns and address people on the basis of that assumption. Sequential thinking takes the form of stating a thesis, offering the major points of proof for that thesis, illustrating the thesis, and drawing a conclusion—thus the three-points-and-a-poem method of preaching. The preacher has a thesis, offers biblical data to support it, illustrates it, and calls for his hearers to draw a certain conclusion or to act in a certain way.

The only problem with this method is that it ignores the reality of our time. As a matter of fact, it may even ignore a fundamental insight from the teaching methods of Jesus himself.

Modern Americans aren't particularly logical and sequential. Before you get to point C, they are already fuzzy about B and completely unaware of A! They think in visual imagery, not in abstractions. They are accustomed to free-standing TV stories, not serials. (Even the soap operas are essentially free-standing. You can drop in and drop out without losing the story line.) And one powerful picture of a starving child on TV will do more to arouse people to send relief aid to a war-torn country than a dozen presidential speeches with charts.

It's time for us to come out of the Dark Ages with regard to communicating with the people in our churches and larger communities. Stories, object lessons, color slides, and videos are not the exclusive possessions of educators, politicians, and advertising agencies. They must be embraced as tools for the church to use in reaching people.

In today's visual culture, a six-minute piece of drama, for example, can have more "punch" in awakening people to their spiritual needs than a forty-minute sermon. A well-done dramatic monologue from Ecclesiastes, the Sermon on the Mount, or the book of Romans can communicate more of the essential message of these textual materials to some people than a four-month sermon series.

One of the most memorable communion experiences I have had in my life happened in our Sunday morning assemblies at Woodmont Hills a couple of years back when twenty or so people dramatized the "Sounds of the Crucifixion" to worshipers sitting with their eyes closed. Men and women exclaimed, "Crucify him!" The sound of the lash on his back brought tears to my eyes. The sound of nails being hammered through his flesh was almost more than I could bear. Then the communion service continued the drama—for the Lord's Supper is experienced as nonliterary symbolism that communicates truth—as we all traveled back together to that distant time and place in eating bread and drinking wine with each other.

Teaching methods like these can evoke different responses in different people. At the end of that particular assembly, two older ladies in our church vowed, "We'll never be back!" On Thursday of the same week, a man in his forties come to my office. With tears flowing down his cheeks, he said, "Since Sunday I have not been able to get the death of Christ out of my mind. It became real to me for the first time while the story was being read. Now I understand how much Jesus loves me and how much I need him. Will you baptize me?" I would hate to think that we have to "trade off" attendees over such events as dramatic readings, but if using such methods helps us reach lost people, don't we need to pursue them?

Sometimes the drama may have a contemporary setting that takes an audience into the skepticism of a university classroom, the tension of a family in crisis, or the confusion of a man or woman in a moral dilemma. Because these are the forms of communication known best by this nonliterary culture that thinks in sound bites rather than sequentially, we must learn to use them for the sake of the gospel message it needs to know.

Our dependence on the lecture/sermon ignores insights from Jesus' way of approaching people. What was his typical method of instruction? Did he preach expository sermons? Did he build extended arguments in precise and formal style? You know he did not.

Our dependence on the lecture/ sermon ignores insights from Jesus' way of approaching people.

Jesus taught principally through interesting stories. I knew the story of the prodigal son before I could read. And an effective story used last Sunday to communicate some spiritual truth will be remembered long after a sermon title or main points have been forgotten. While I love expository preaching, Jesus only rarely used anything resembling it—and that in spite of his own and his hearers' familiarity with the Law, Prophets, and Psalms. He talked about flowers, farmers, sheep, and vineyards. He told engaging stories from life that had a kingdom meaning.

We are no longer an agrarian culture. Thus our world is one where "the essentially rural values of status quo, sameness, harmony, smallness, and establishment" have yielded to the "urban values of change, diversity, conflict management, bigness, and mobility."[8] And I have no doubt that if he were to come and teach personally in our time, Jesus would do so with this awareness. He would use stories appropriate to a world of cyberspace and virtual-reality technology. He would be well-versed in current events. He would wrap truth in the events of time and place. If Aristotelian argument forms had been more effective than simple stories, he would have used them. The fact that he used a simpler method ought to teach us something about methodology.

Our Use of Music

A second area where we must broaden our horizons and be more biblical than traditional is with our use of music. Allan Bloom has insisted that music is the most powerful influence in the lives of people today. "Though students do not have books, they most emphatically do have music. . . . It is their passion; nothing else excites them as it does; they cannot take seriously anything alien to music."[9]

If you lived through your teen years prior to the 1960s, you probably think of music as background noise and "filler." So you may turn on the radio while doing housework or driving. For the post-sixties crowd, however, music means much more. It is central to and defines their lifestyle.

For people who grew up during the sixties, music was their medium of truth. When politicians were lying to them about Vietnam, institutions were resisting racial equality, and parents were behaving hypocritically about drugs and alcohol, their music was the one source they could trust. They made it their special province.

And now churches wonder aloud about losing younger members from the church and about our inability to evangelize our culture. Why do people who grow up among us lose interest in the church? Why do so many who still come show no real enthusiasm for worship? Why are non-Christians not drawn to our corporate worship?

Maybe the answer is *idolatry*. Whenever a generation presumes that its way of doing a thing is the only way to do it with the blessing of God, that is a not-so-subtle form of idolatry. Many of the preachers and elders from the pre-sixties generation insist that no formula for writing and choosing church music can be used other than the one that was contrived for their generation.

Older people with a taste for classical music love the stately words and conventional music of "O Sacred Head" or "Joyful, Joyful We Adore Thee." Others of that generation may prefer the Stamps-Baxter songs like "Farther Along" or "Just a Little Talk with Jesus." They neither know nor appreciate the musical tastes of a younger generation whose music is totally different.

If *either* generation refuses to allow for the other, it makes an idol of itself, its preferences, and its tastes. A church that cannot bridge the gap in these issues, so as to allow all generations to share in the life of the church, will never be capable of dealing with the really major spiritual issues of our time and fails to be faithful to our divine calling to be "all things to all men" (1 Cor. 9:22).

Our View on Female Participation

A third area where our received tradition limits us needlessly has to do with female participation in corporate worship. My views on female leadership of corporate worship are quite conservative. My opinion is that the New Testament prohibits one office and two functions to Christian women in the church's life. I understand that the office of elder/presbyter/overseer is reserved for males; I understand that sessions of prayer and teaching/preaching of the Word of God in the church's corporate worship are to be directed by Christian males. But I also believe we are wrong to bury the talents of women in all other aspects of the church's life. Many seem to think the "safe course" is to continue prohibiting women from doing things in the life of the church that have been off-limits for them because of cultural mores. Since these prohibitions arose from culture, they should vanish in the church as cultural changes occur around us.

> The Bible is not against women ministering, using their God-given talents, standing up and speaking, administering church programs, singing (congregationally, small groups, or solo), reading Scripture, sharing information about church projects, testifying, teaching sub-groups of the church's membership (whether female, male, or mixed), writing articles or poems, or otherwise participating fully in the life of local churches. A church's failure to encourage the development of female talent robs it of countless blessings. That same failure results in buried talents that return no dividend to the owner who entrusted them to the church through its female membership.[10]

The difference between females preaching and leading prayers for the assembly and these service roles is the difference between directing the group on one's own initiative and ministering to it in a predetermined way. In the former, one chooses the course for the group and genuinely leads/guide it; in the latter, one follows a text and interprets it to the group. It is simply not true that every instance of standing and speaking before a group involves taking charge of or giving guidance to that group.

The larger issue of the role of women in the life of the church is more than I want to address here, but our traditions in corporate worship do need examination. Such an examination is not an abandonment of the Word of God but is necessary for a faithful application of the Word of God to our time and place.

Conclusion

Two Catholic priests were walking down a corridor together twenty-five years ago. One said, "Ah, the beauty of the Latin Mass! God forbid that these 'liberals' and 'trouble-makers' desecrate it with the vulgar languages of mankind."

"Is it our task to preserve what we have known or to communicate the message of Christ faithfully to our generation?"

"But must we not be concerned that what happens in our churches and cathedrals be intelligible to those who enter?" asked the other. "Is it our task to preserve the Latin Mass or to speak a meaningful message to our parishioners?"

Two preachers were talking together at a conference this year. One said, "Ah, the beauty of the King James Version, Stamps-Baxter music, and all other elements of our worship! God forbid that these 'liberals' and 'trouble-makers' desecrate our services with dialogue sermons, Michael Card songs, or drama."

"But must we not be concerned that what happens in our churches and lectureships be intelligible to those who enter?" asked the other. "Is it our task to preserve what we have known or to communicate the message of Christ faithfully to our generation?"

Paul was concerned about the Corinthian church's attachment to tongue-speaking, when a nobler concern should have been prophecy—with love, I might add, guiding both. Tongue-speaking was proper, he insisted, but it could become a hindrance to communication with unbelievers. It takes very little imagination to recast his words on that point to our own time and situation.

> So if the whole church comes together and everyone speaks in tongues [or the worship styles of a century ago], and some who do not understand or some unbelievers come in, will they not say that you are out of your mind? But if an unbeliever or someone who does not understand comes in while everybody is prophesying [celebrating God in ways that communicate with these "uninitiated folk" who don't know King James jargon, older musical styles, or out-of-touch teaching methods], he will be convinced by all that he is a sinner and will be judged by all, and the secrets of his heart will be laid bare. So he will fall down and worship God, exclaiming, "God is really among you!" (1 Cor. 14:23–25)

So let me repeat: *worship that is not relevant is not biblical.* Worship so dated in style and method that it is remote from our contemporaries must be seen for the handicap to communication it is. As we exalt our God in worship, our goal must be to connect with people rather than bemuse them with period-piece worship styles.

The wonder (i.e., awe, reverence, submission) that ought to be sensed in our corporate worship is the wonder that comes of divine encounter and causes even non-Christians to say "God is really among you!" instead of the confused "I wonder (i.e., am confused about) what all this means" that arises when a (culturally) foreign language is spoken in the presence of—but out of touch with—the worshiping community that has assembled.

---

1. *New International Dictionary of New Testament Theology*, 1976 ed., s.v. *"proskyneo,"* by Hans Schonweiss and Colin Brown.

2. *International Standard Bible Encyclopedia*, 1988 ed., s.v. "Worship," by Ralph P. Martin.

3. Mark Horst, "Worship's Focus: Seeking the Face of God," *Christian Century*, 11 November 1987, 991.

4. Ralph P. Martin, *The Worship of God* (Grand Rapids: William B. Eerdmans Publishing Co., 1982), 183–4.

5. Dan Scott, *The Emerging American Church* (Anderson, Ind.: Briston Books, 1993), 271.

6. Jaroslav Pelikan, "Christianity as an Enfolding Circle," *U.S. News & World Report*, 26 June 1989, 57.

7. George G. Hunter III, *How to Reach Secular People* (Nashville: Abingdon Press, 1992).

8. Russell Chandler, *Racing Toward 2001* (Grand Rapids: Zondervan Publishing House, 1992), 20.

9. Allan Bloom, *The Closing of the American Mind* (New York: Simon and Schuster, 1987), 68.

10. Rubel Shelly, "A Woman's Place Is . . . ," *Wineskins*, May 1993, 5.

DR. HAROLD SHANK

◆

The Other Six Days

Worship and Ethics

CHAPTER FIVE

He had never gone to church before in his life, but after six weeks of attending our congregation, he told me that while he didn't always understand the language we used and often failed to grasp the significance of what we did, one thing was clear: the more he came to church, the more he felt his life was wrong. He concluded he had to either change his life or change what he did on Sunday. He changed his life.

A middle-age woman, who had attended church for years, came to tell me she would not be back. Sunday morning offered her no connection to the rest of the week. The routine of Sunday seemed too far removed from the realities of Monday. What especially appalled her were people who talked about one kind of life and lived another. The hypocrisy, in others and herself, was too much. She left.

One drawn. One repelled. One convicted to change. Another moved to leave. One saw the connection between Sunday and the other six days. The other saw no link between church and life.

These two people raise a critical question: What is the relationship between our worship in the Sunday assembly and our ethical behavior the other six days? Is what we do on Sunday relevant to the rest of our lives? Theologically speaking, how do worship and ethics relate?

To respond to this inquiry, two initial steps are necessary. First, we must define terms. Words like *worship, assembly,* and *ethics* have a broad range of meanings in the English language. For the sake of clarity, this chapter will use *worship* when discussing the individual's intense response of love and devotion to God and the term *assembly* when referring to the Sunday gatherings of the church when members of the spiritual community join together in their worship of God. The term *ethics* refers to the living of the Christian life, either individually or congregationally.

Second, we must clarify the issue. The relationship between worship and ethics can be framed in two significant ways:

- Does worship affect individual or congregational ethics?

- Do the ethics of an individual or congregation affect their worship?

Thus the focus of this chapter is not simply the nature of worship or the nature of ethics, but an exploration of how the two relate. As their relationship becomes clearer, the nature of both worship and ethics will come into focus.

Does Worship Affect Ethics?

William Willimon's volume, *The Service of God*, asks, "Does a Christian's worship make any real difference to a Christian's moral life?"[1] Does the church find ethical prompting from its Sunday gatherings?

In practice, if not in theology, the church has answered *yes*. Willimon joins with the host of Christendom in observing that we have adopted this principle without much reflection. Prayers move people to action, sermons motivate the church to ministry, and songs convict us about our service to God. Most would agree that something happens in Sunday assembly that prompts Monday service.[2]

The Focus of Worship Is God

Yet, as Willimon observes, we should be careful not to say or believe that we worship God in order to be better people. He argues that we can keep the focus of worship on God without severing any relationship between worship and ethics. The purpose of worship is not to prompt ethical behavior but to praise God.

For example, the depictions of worship in Revelation place the focus on God. The worshipers sing and pay homage simply because they are in the presence of God. There is no sense of being there to improve their ethics, but they spend eternity responding in love to the majestic presence of God.

We worship God, not self-improvement. Even the definition of worship, as adoration, homage, or praise toward God, excludes an ethical segment. Our worship comes as a response to his love and grace. Worship is fundamentally God-centered.[3]

If the purpose of worship centers around our response to God, how can we speak of worship changing life?[4] How does the worship we offer while in Sunday assembly affect our lives? The issue calls for a theological discussion of how ethics and worship relate.

The Theological Link Between Ethics and Worship

Scripture Relates Them by the Words Used

First, Scripture itself relates ethics and worship by the words it uses. Several Hebrew and Greek words are translated "worship" or "service." In at least one case in Hebrew and one in Greek, the word for *service* refers either to worship or ethics. The same Hebrew root (*'abad*) describes the Israelites' worship at Sinai (Exod. 3:12), their work in Egypt (Exod. 5:9), and their slavery in Egypt (Exod. 1:13). The same Greek word (*leitourgia*) used of Zechariah's worship in the temple (Luke 1:23) and the Corinthians' gift to God (2 Cor. 9:12) also describes the work Epaphroditus did for God (Phil. 2:30).

English speakers reflect a similar span of meaning when we use the same word to refer to service on Sunday, our service to the ill when we visit the hospital, and what we do when we offer service at a soup kitchen.

Theologically, a link exists between the praise God receives from what we do and the praise God receives from what we sing.

While an individual or a spiritual community often takes specific times to focus more directly on God, Scripture informs us that all our lives are service to him. Romans 12:1–2 demands our bodies (ethics) as a living sacrifice, which then becomes our spiritual service (worship). Clearly the food service in the soup kitchen differs in substantial ways from the worship service on Sunday, but Christians seek to glorify God in both kinds of service. Theologically, a link exists between the praise God receives from what we do and the praise God receives from what we sing. We honor God by the words of our prayer and by the works of our hands. We remember God by partaking of the Lord's Supper and by the way we remember his special people, the weak. We glorify God by giving our money and our time.

We might imagine a theological outline: service to God is a general category, and the different kinds of service are subcategories. One kind of service is worship; another kind is financial giving; still another part of our service to God is our compassion for the weak and poor.

Service
    a. Worship
    b. Giving
    c. Compassion

In using this illustration, I do not mean to form rigid lines and airtight categories. I only mean to illustrate that worship, giving, and compassion have a way of linking our worship and our ethics. This allows us to make sense of the ways in which the Bible uses the words and texts like Romans 12:1–2, which provide the link between worship and ethics.

Scripture Relates Them by Their Juxtaposition

Second, Scripture relates worship and ethics by their juxtaposition in the same text. Matthew gives us a glimpse of a link between worship and ethics:

> Then the eleven disciples went to Galilee, to the mountain where Jesus had told them to go. When they saw him, they worshiped him; but some doubted. Then Jesus came to them and said, "All authority in heaven and on earth has been given to me. Therefore go and make disciples of all nations, baptizing them in the name of the Father and of the Son and of the Holy Spirit, and teaching them to obey everything I have commanded you. And surely I am with you always, to the very end of the age." (Matt. 28:16–20)

This postresurrection text combines the worship of the disciples with the command about how they are to live (ethics). The text does not describe the link between worship and ethics but merely places the two side by side.

More extensive links are found in two of the Bible's primary texts on worship: Deuteronomy and Psalms.

Deuteronomy centers its instruction around the core commands about love.[5] The Ten Commandments (Deut. 5) outline the broad ways in which Israel can love God and neighbor. The statutes and ordinances in Deuteronomy 12–26 offer specific case studies and particular instructions about living a life of love. Among the specific topics discussed in Deuteronomy 12–26 are the proper worship of God[6] and the proper care of the needy and the weak.[7] These two central topics in Deuteronomy again bring together worship and ethics (proper care of the needy and weak). In starting a new nation, the Law of Moses outlines how a perfect spiritual community would function. In order to build this ideal community, the law calls for both worship and ethics. Without either one, the community falls short of God's plan. Indeed, Deuteronomy 16 insists that all members of the community—including the poor—be allowed to participate in the worship. Like the Matthew 28 text, Scripture lays the topics of worship and ethics side by side. While few stated links exist, Deuteronomy implies that the way Israel worshiped and the way Israel treated the poor were both essential to God's plan.

The Psalms make up a second primary Old Testament worship text. The 150 pieces of Hebrew poetry provide God-inspired words to use in worship. Ethics and worship appear linked in Psalm 1, which reminds the reader that God sees a connection between the one who meditates on the law (worship) and the one who walks by the law (ethics). The rest of the Psalter regularly mingles worship and ethics. Texts expressing worship to God are scattered throughout. Passages that call for attention to the weak and poor include Psalm 41:1, which asks God to bless those who help the poor. Psalm 72:13 teaches us that God has pity on the poor and weak. Psalm 82:1–4 calls God to work justice and rescue the weak and oppressed. Psalm 113:7 anticipates God's work on behalf of the poor. Throughout Psalms, God speaks about the widows and orphans[8] and about the oppressed.[9] In Psalms, ethics is not divorced from worship. Messages about ethical concerns for these groups repeatedly surface in the Psalms, offering solid evidence of the link between worship and ethics.

By both the words it uses and the juxtaposition of worship and ethical texts, Scripture assumes, as do we, some connection between the worship we offer and the service we give.

Do Ethics
Affect Worship?

Willimon's question, "Does a Christian's worship make any real difference to a Christian's moral life?" presupposes a second inquiry: "Does a Christian's moral life make any real difference to a Christian's worship?" Does a congregation's ministry make any difference in their corporate worship? Do ethics affect worship?

Churches obviously differ. Members of one church, for example, brought handicapped children to the Sunday assembly, but the church leaders asked them not to come back because they "disturbed the worship." Members of another congregation started a program for handicapped children. Their leaders urged them to come.

One church built a parking lot, put in curbs and gutters, and erected a sign reading, "Church Parking Only." After another group constructed a new parking area, they encouraged commuters to leave their cars there during the day.

One church met in a transitional community. They put new locks on the doors and installed a security system. Another church responded to the changing neighborhood by leaving the church doors open so people could come to a quiet place.

When a different race of people moved into the neighborhood, one congregation put up a "For Sale" sign, while another group greeted the people of a different race with a welcome mat.

Seeing the crime rate go up made one group move to the suburbs. Another church, alarmed at the increase in violence, decided to plant a church in the most dangerous area.

The issue raised by each of these examples is whether or not these various ethical behaviors affect the congregation's Sunday assembly: Does ethical behavior affect worship?

A visit to the Sunday services of any of these churches might not be terribly revealing. The songs, sermons, and prayers of congregations involved in godly ethical behavior might differ little from groups neglecting the work of God. An individual whose life reflects none of God's ethical demands may even offer a more spirited and heartfelt worship than the godly person on the next pew. Should we conclude ethics has no affect on worship? Scripture goes in another direction.

Scripture Links Ethics to Worship

In 1 Samuel 15, Saul prepared for worship by picking out the best Amalekite livestock to sacrifice at the tabernacle. But before he arrived at the church door, God rejected his worship, his praise of God negated by a life of disobedience. Samuel warned, "To obey is better than sacrifice."

Isaiah, Hosea, Amos, and Micah tell how the Judeans filled the temple with the sounds of sacrificed sheep, holy feasts, and heartfelt praise.[10] But God wasn't listening. Instead of their praise, God heard the cries of the fatherless child. Instead of their prayers, he listened to the anguish of the oppressed underclass. Instead of hearing the woman in the temple with hands held high, he heard the widow in poverty with hands held low.

Instead of their praise, God heard the cries of the fatherless child.

In Matthew 5, Jesus said that anyone offering a gift to God must first be right with his brother. In essence, he said, "If you're not right with your brother, God will not accept your worship. Reunite with your brother, then unite with God."

John defines God as love (1 John 3–4). He calls us to love God. Can there be any simpler definition of worship than to ask somebody to love God? Yet John will not acknowledge love of God apart from active concern for a friend in need. No amount of talk about love to God, no amount of words on Sunday about love for God can negate the glaring failure to help a brother in need.

The relationship between worship and ethics is especially striking in Amos 5:

I hate, I despise your feasts, and I take no delight in your solemn assemblies. Even though you offer me your burnt offerings and cereal offerings, I will not accept them, and the peace offerings of your fatted beasts I will not look upon. Take away from me the noise of your songs; to the melody of your harps I will not listen. But let justice roll down like waters, and righteousness like an ever-flowing stream. (Amos 5:21–24 RSV)

This passage evaluates worship and ethics. Today, human evaluation of Sunday assemblies often takes place around the Sunday dinner table as participants critique the sermon, the singing, the prayers, and other activities of the assembly. Amos offers God's response to the service. The Israelite family that attended service at the Samaritan temple may have criticized the sacrifices or the music, or they may have praised the homily or the procession, but nothing compares to God's critique recorded by Amos.

First, notice the seven *descriptions* of Israelite worship from the Amos 5 passage:[11]

1. *Feasts* refers to the three Israelite celebrations of worship: Passover, Pentecost, and Tabernacles.

2. *Solemn assemblies* describes their regular gatherings.

3. *Burnt offerings* refers to the animal sacrifices.

4. *Cereal offerings* were grain sacrifices presented in the temple.

5. *Peace offerings* were animal sacrifices that were subsequently enjoyed as a meal.

6. *Noise* is a reference to singing.

7. *Melody* probably refers to the instrumental music in the temple area.

God's description of Israelite worship covers the entire spectrum. He references the time, the words, the sacrifices, and the music. God omits no part of their worship.

Second, God has six *reactions* to Israelite worship:

1. I hate it.

2. I despise it.

3. I take no delight in it (this phrase is literally "I don't like the smell of it").

4. I will not accept it.

5. I will not look on it.

6. I will not listen to it.

God doesn't like how it smells, how it looks, or how it sounds. If his description of Israelite worship was comprehensive, his rejection of it is equally exhaustive. The heavenly response to Israelite worship was complete: "I do not like anything you do. I do not want to hear anything you say."

Why was God so angry with the Israelite worship? He was angry because they had isolated themselves from the poor. He objected to their seeking other gods. He was incensed that they abused and cheated other people. He hated the way they ignored his commandments.

God Calls Us to Justice and Righteousness

Instead of their outward show of ceremony, God called the Israelites to participate in justice and righteousness. *Justice* and *righteousness* appear together in the Hebrew Bible ninety-eight times. Justice fixes on treating people fairly. Righteousness is the quality of the person who treats another fairly. Justice emphasizes fairness and equity. Righteousness stresses kindness and generosity. Together they form a powerful Old Testament team. Justice and righteousness are qualities of God. As people focus on a just and righteous God, he expects them to take on those qualities. He expects his people to interfere in the affairs of others to ensure justice and righteousness. All through the Hebrew Bible, writers talk about the inevitability of justice and righteousness. They will triumph. To block justice or righteousness is to oppose God himself. Followers of God do not bring about justice or righteousness; they only choose whether to participate in God's ever flowing stream or to wither on the bank.

Instead of their outward show of ceremony, God called the Israelites to participate in justice and righteousness.

First Samuel 15, Isaiah 1, Micah 6, Hosea 6, Matthew 5, 1 John 3–4, and Amos 5 tell us about a fundamental biblical concern: the link between ethics and worship. If the worshipers have no concern for the issues that matter to God, God will not hear their worship. Worshipers unfamiliar with these texts may not even know of God's rejection. Observers at their worship periods could be equally unaware of the absence of God. Despite the lack of empirical evidence of God's rejection, these texts make it clear that the ethical behavior of individuals and communities directly affects God's reception of their worship.

These texts add one crucial factor to the relationship between obedience and worship which may be widely overlooked in the current discussions of worship. The link between ethics and worship is critical. Our praise on Sunday is rejected if we have not sought to please him on Friday.

These texts reveal that God expects both obedience and worship. Worship without obedience fails to be worship.[12] Such connections do not sit well with us. We do not like to be told that our worship is not acceptable; we prefer to make our own judgments about worship. We have been told that if our hearts are right in worship, God will accept it. God certainly expects right hearts in worship, but Scripture makes it clear that right lives must also be in place before worship can be acceptable to God. The text in John speaks clearly: "If anyone has material possessions and sees his brother in need but has no pity on him, how can the love of God be in him?" (1 John 3:17). We might insist that a person who does not help his brother can still love God. But John denies it. God demands continuity between what we do and what we say.

The Assembly Prompts Both Worship and Ethics

Willimon brings yet another perspective to the discussion. Rather than making ethics the by-product of worship, he observes that both worship and ethics arise as a response to the assembly.

Acts 2:41–47 and 4:23–31 report on assemblies of the infant church. When they gathered, they listened to the apostles' teaching, they strengthened their fellowship, they ate the Lord's Supper, and they prayed. As a result, they praised God, spoke the word of God boldly, and extended compassion to all who had need.

The assembly prompted both worship and ethics. their experiences in church led them to praise God and to act in new ways, reflecting the ethical call of the new movement.

Willimon outlines six possible ways in which the assembly can create both worship and ethics.

1. Sunday assemblies often rehearse the God-human story to remind us of what God has done as a means of moving us to a worship response. These rehearsals also have the effect of renewing our sense of identity as Christians in the world. Revival of our identity has profound implications for our practice. The same rehearsal thus produces both a worship and ethical response.

2. Sunday services bring us into God's world, prompting us to reflect on God's reality through worship. Reentering God's world not only leads us to worship, but it also reshapes us as individuals, giving us a new sense of direction.

3. Our corporate worship helps us make sense of the world by reminding us of sin, salvation, and human freedom to choose between God and evil. Not only does that awareness turn us toward God, but it also prompts ethical renewal.

4. Sunday gives us hope. Scripture itself allows us to imagine a different future than the one we contemplate when separated from God's word. Not only does this draw us to our creator, but it alters our self-view as creation. Hope has worship and ethical implications.

5. Our joint focus on God reminds us about God's solutions to the world's problems. Not only do we celebrate his resolution, but we see also the implications for our own lives. If not for Sunday service, we might not know what was wrong with our world. Sunday service reminds us that the world will be saved by a man on a cross, not a man with a credit card.

6. Worshiping God together reminds us of our common past. Knowing that, as worshipers, we join a long list of others bowed before his throne keeps us keenly aware of the unbroken way God has blessed his people. We leave with a sense of relationship with the past that makes us live our days in altered ways. Knowing that our fathers worshiped the same God gives us a basis for future living.[13]

An example of Willimon's point is seen when the disciples bowed before Jesus (worship) on the mountain and wanted to serve him (ethics) as a result of being in his presence. Almost any of the six points suggested by Willimon could have prompted the disciples' response.

Just as one customer's phone call to the Federal Express agent prompts a message to a driver to pickup a package, a computer command to send that customer a bill, and an entry into the system that tracks the package from pickup to delivery, so this analysis suggests that certain theological issues flow from each other. When an individual or congregation reflects for any period of time on the God-human story, several responses are expected. One is worship. Another is ethical behavior. Both flow from the same source.

Reflection on God in the assembly

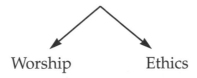

Worship   Ethics

Such a chart does not reflect all there is to say about worship or ethics, nor does it imply that these lines reflect rigid theological categories. Rather, it outlines a helpful way of tracking how the assembly prompts both worship and ethics.

Worshiping God in Spite of Ethical Failures

Given our constant failures at living God's ethical standards, how can anyone worship God? Three points will help clarify this issue.

First, worship and ethics must be kept on the right side of grace. We do not worship in order to be saved, nor do we live right in order to be saved. Both worship and ethics are a response to the grace of God. We worship because we are saved. We attempt a Christian ethic because of God's mercy in our lives. Salvation comes by the mercy of God, not because we participate in God's crusade for righteousness and justice. But in response to God's salvation, he expects obedience and worship.

Second, pay attention to the biblical teachings on ethical behavior. Since God has made his ethical concerns clear, we cannot plead ignorance. Isaiah wrote: "Seek justice, encourage the oppressed. Defend the cause of the fatherless, plead the case of the widow" (Isa. 1:17).

God's commands throughout Scripture cannot be missed or ignored. James wrote, "Religion that God our Father accepts as pure and faultless is this: to look after orphans and widows in their distress and to keep oneself from being polluted by the world" (James 1:27).

We cannot ignore these demands any more than we can neglect the texts about worship. God has linked the two. In response to God's grace, we must take up his agenda for our lives. God's rejection of worship is directed at those who completely ignore God's ethical demands. He refuses to listen to worship of people who refuse to listen to his commands. If we refuse to listen, we stand judged by these texts.

The ultimate intent of Scripture is not to shame us, but to inspire us.

Most of us do not fall into the category of people who have refused to heed God's commands. We have not taken matters into our own hands like Saul did. We have not ignored our brothers in need. We have not ignored the widow and orphan. The message to us is not that God is not listening, but a reminder that we worship a God who not only listens to our praise, but who also watches our practice.

Third, call on God's power of transformation. The ultimate intent of Scripture is not to shame us, but to inspire us. We should not feel pushed down, but astonished at how God has lifted us up. Theology is not ultimately oppressive, but suggestive; not burdensome, but winsome; not defeating, but invigorating. So I want to emphasize not that we are bad and can do no good, but that we are saved and loved by God. We must not hide from the clear teachings of the word of God regarding worship and ethics, but neither should we conceal ourselves from the richness of his power and the greatness of his ability to transform. I believe that as individuals and as churches, we can live the kinds of lives God calls us to and that we can offer him the kind of worship that brings a smile to his face and satisfaction to his heart.

The Link between Worship and Ethics Demonstrated

God's link between worship and ethics is constantly being lived out. I close with three recent experiences of the link between our lives and our Sunday assemblies. Dave came before the church to make a few comments about the Lord's Supper. I had trouble concentrating on his words because I was so struck by his transformation. I'd been to his house. I knew his story. Six months earlier he had been in prison after beating his wife beyond recognition. Everybody in the family had feared this broad-shouldered, muscular, ex-Navy Seal. His imprisonment had given the family relief. His mother-in-law had sold all his possessions, hoping he would die in prison. People from church had tried to keep the family intact. Everybody feared his return. But six months is a long time, time enough for God to change a man.

A few weeks before this particular church service, in Dave's neighborhood, another man beat his girlfriend. Kicking her out of the house at 4 A.M., he blamed her for not having enough money to support his drug habit. A few minutes later, the girl ran into four men on the street. They abused her more. She returned home to her boyfriend, who put her back outside with a contemptuous, "You did this to yourself." In those early morning hours she met Dave, the God-changed ex-con. After one look, he knew what had happened to her because he had inflicted the same pain on his own wife. He listened for two hours as she poured out her story. The next morning, he took her to the church, helped find her shelter, and located some women to help her clean up. When his own wife came home from her night job, he brought the two women together. He knew his wife's experience would help the battered girl.

And now he stood before the church, huge trembling hands holding a simple plate of bread, his heart filled with gratitude to God for the change in his life. Then he gently lifted the juice, reflecting not only on the blood he had shed, but the blood shed for him. I was moved— awed by the change God had brought in Dave's life, moved by the way he led us all in worship.

Dave reminds us all that when we yield to God, he works with us and we respond in worship. None of us is too far gone. Not one of us is beyond the mighty hand of God. There is no man or woman beyond the changing power of God.

Furthermore, no church is beyond God's mighty hand. I was recently at a Sunday service in Memphis when a woman opened the door, walked down the aisle, and approached the preacher. She started swearing, complaining, and demanding. She talked so fast that I couldn't understand what she wanted. After a few minutes, the preacher guided her out of the room. By the time the song leader finished directing us in a song, the preacher returned to finish his lesson as if nothing had happened.

Later I asked the minister about the incident. Rita has the mind of an eight-year-old. Sometimes she gets upset when she can't get what she wants. On rare occasions, like the scene I witnessed, she becomes loud and boisterous. Normally, she attends church without incident.

Rita's occasional offensive behavior forced that congregation to make a decision about worship and ethics. Her rude behavior bothered many, yet they knew that Rita would not be allowed to attend most churches. They discussed whether Rita should be loved and accepted or put out. They decided to love her. As a result, she attends regularly. They have decided that, on the rare occasions when she becomes disruptive, they will let her walk on them enough to let her know they love her, and then gently lead her to where she needs to be.

When we yield to God, he works with us. None of us is too far gone.

Rather than an invasion of their worship, Rita has become part of their assembly. Their treatment of an outcast from society has formed them into the kingdom of God. By not excluding her, God has included them. Amos was right. Justice rolls like waters and righteousness like ever flowing streams.

A battered woman called 911 in Fort Worth. The police officer who answered the call found her on the verge of suicide. After calming her troubled emotions, he told her he knew of some people who could help. He took her to the Richland Hills Church of Christ. He just knew they would help. They did. They talked to her. They provided housing. They helped her restart life.

As her story unfolded, they learned she had come from mainland China, married an American, and found herself a battered wife. The officer who helped her didn't attend the Richland Hills church, but he knew of their reputation as a helping community. After they took care of the woman's immediate needs, they learned that although she had lived in Fort Worth for over a year, she had never seen a Bible. One thing led to another. She became a Christian.

This church also sponsors World Bible Translation Center. At about the same time the 911 call came in, they began looking for a native speaker to assist them with a translation of the Bible into Chinese. The woman who called 911 became a Christian, was hired by the church, and helped produce a Bible in her own language.

Not long ago the church invited this Chinese Christian woman and the police officer to their Sunday morning assembly. The story was told. A copy of the new Chinese Bible was shown. The church responded by giving God praise for what had been done.

Praise cannot be ripped away from obedience. The same settings that prompt worship encourage ethics. Homage to God cannot be isolated from the way we treat others. When justice flows like a river, praise will tumble out like a waterfall. When righteousness becomes an ever flowing stream, worship will be a never ending result.

1. William Willimon, *The Service of God* (Nashville: Abingdon, 1983), 15. Willimon uses the term *worship* to refer to the assembly on Sunday.

2. Not all agree. For example, Daniel Berrigan writes, "No one has been able to demonstrate that Christian worship leads, in any large or direct sense, to Christian conduct in the world." "I Lift My Eyes to You, My Help, My Hope: Psalms and Meditation," *The Catholic Worker* 42 (December 1976), 4.

3. Willimon, *Service of God*, 42.

4. The ethical issue of whether Sunday assemblies should be used to motivate ethical behavior is being excluded from this study. Such a discussion lies within the purpose of the Sunday assembly and the nature of worship.

5. See Deut. 6:4–5; 7:6–11; 10:12–22. On this treatment of Deuteronomy, see Patrick D. Miller, "The Way of Torah," *Princeton Seminary Bulletin* 8 (1987), 17–27.

6. See Deut. 12:1–32; 14:22–29; 15:19–23; 16:1–17; 17:1.

7. See Deut. 15:1–22; 16:13–20.

8. See Pss. 10:14, 18; 68:5; 78:65; 94:6; 109:9, 12; 146:9.

9. See Pss. 9:9; 10:18; 62:10; 72:4; 74:21; 103:6; 119:134; 146:7.

10. Isa. 1:12–17; Hos. 6:6; 8:13; Amos 5:21–24; Mic. 6:6–8.

11. This section is informed by James Limburg, *Hosea-Micah* (Interpretation; Atlanta: John Knox, 1988), 104–9.

12. The issue of obedience without worship is outside the general flow of this study. Ethics cannot be practiced without worship any more than worship can be maintained without ethics.

13. Willimon, *Service of God*, 48–72.

DR. JACK R. REESE

◆

One Bright Chain of Loving Rite

Water, Bread, and Wine

CHAPTER SIX

You could almost feel the panic in his eyes. Maybe it wasn't panic. Astonishment? Alarm? Confusion? Shock? Whatever it was, he was certainly not prepared for what happened in the auditorium that morning.

My friend, Roger, was sitting through a service unlike anything he had experienced before. He had not known exactly what to expect, but he had not expected this. First of all, he was a little taken aback that the men and women sat in separate sections. He had really wanted to sit by his wife, but apparently that was taboo.

But then when the participants started their chanting—low, rumbling, indecipherable—his blood ran cold.

Roger was ready to bolt for the door. This was the weirdest thing he had ever seen.

Larry, the friend who had brought him to the service, was really getting into it. Eyes closed. Hands raised, palms down. The chanting began to crescendo, and many in the crowd seemed almost in a trance.

And then, the most bizarre thing: one of the leaders of the group stood up and began to describe in vivid detail the ceremony he had participated in as a young man, blood rites that initiated him into the group. Larry, almost unconsciously, fingered the scar on his wrist, apparently remembering his own rite of passage into the ancient Order of the Cruxifarians.

Then, suddenly, as if by an unseen cue, everyone around him jumped to their feet, raised their hands, and screamed, "Hoy Yomach. Hoy Ramach."

No, *panic* was the right word. Roger was ready to bolt for the door. This was the weirdest thing he had ever seen.

Outsiders See Our "Rites" as Bizarre

Okay, you're right. That's a made-up story. But it does provide a hint as to how utterly strange some of the things are that *we* do in church. I mean, in the eyes of some outsiders, *the stuff we do is no less bizarre.*

I'm not just talking about why a "fool" would go to church on Sundays instead of sleeping in, reading the entire Sunday edition of the *New York Times,* or playing golf like most "normal" people. The strangeness I am describing is more than that. When you became a Christian, you did a remarkably peculiar thing. You stepped into a tank of water, somebody said a few words, and you were dunked under. Why would anybody do that? Do you really think something happened? People submerge themselves under water all the time—they bathe, they swim—but nothing divine happens. Why would any intelligent person consent to be thrust under water as a sign of his or her belief?

And then, this Sunday you will probably do what you do most weeks. It's no big deal, really. It's almost incidental. You will take a tiny piece of cracker and eat it. Then you will drink a sip of grape juice from a little cup. In church. I'm here to tell you, that's strange.

It is so odd, when you stop and think about it, that no one was shocked several years ago when a minister at a prominent church declared, "The Lord's Supper is confusing to our guests. More than that, it's the most boring part of Sunday worship. Therefore, we try to do it quickly—in less than eight minutes if possible—in order to get on to more exciting and enjoyable things like singing and a good sermon."

Nor is it surprising that some evangelical churches avoid taking communion on Sundays. They are aggressively seeking the unchurched, which of course is commendable, and since such rituals are strange to unchurched people, the Lord's Supper is simply not served during Sunday morning "seeker services."

Of course, this is not the first time in the history of Christianity that outsiders have been repulsed or confused by such practices. The earliest Christians found themselves constantly opposed by the pagans because of their bizarre customs. Christians, after all, were committing incest. (They called each other "brother" and "sister," did they not?) And they practiced outright cannibalism. (Every week in their secret ceremonies they "ate the flesh and drank the blood of their god.")

No, it really shouldn't surprise us that outsiders find these practices strange. They have from the very beginning.

Something Happens
in the Ceremony

The significance of baptism and the Lord's Supper lies not in the rituals themselves but in the work of God in them. Something actually *happens* in these ceremonies. I illustrate this with the following scenes from my own experience.

One of my most poignant memories is of my friend Jim Martin baptizing his oldest son, Jeremy. There were few dry eyes in the house as we waited for him to baptize his boy. Jim addressed his son, "Jeremy, when you were born, your mother and I gave thanks to God for this precious gift. And we made a commitment to God that just as he had given you to us at your birth, we would someone give you back to him. Today is that day."

I believe that those were not just sweet thoughts from a sentimental father. I believe they convey the reality that something actually happens in baptism. It is not just a completion of steps. Something divine occurs.

I am not saying that there is power in the baptismal waters to take away sins. The power of baptism is in the Savior, not the water. The work of baptism is God's work, not ours. God does the saving. Our baptism is a participation in the blood of Christ, which alone has the power to save us.

But something happens in baptism. An old person dies; a new person rises. The one who was not a Christian becomes a Christian; she is forgiven, a new creature in a new relationship. And the Holy Spirit is given as a gift. Something actually happens. In the tears, joy, and hugs, we believe a soul has been snatched away from Satan. We believe baptism works!

The second scene happened years earlier when I was a teenager. For thirteen weeks, our high school Sunday School class studied Christian doctrine (something I can hardly imagine in many of today's churches). One of the weeks was devoted to the Lord's Supper. Among other things, we were told what we were to do during the taking of the Lord's Supper. Primarily we were to remember ("Do this in remembrance of me"). We were instructed to "think about Jesus."

The significance of baptism and the Lord's Supper lies not in the rituals themselves but in the work of God in them.

"Does anything happen during the Lord's Supper?" one student asked. "I mean, does God do anything to us?"

"No," we were told. "Nothing happens. It's just a time to think about Jesus."

"Why do we do it, then?"

"Because of biblical example. According to Acts 20:7 'On the first day of the week, the disciples gathered together to break bread.' They did it, so we have to do it that way."

We have believed that God works in baptism, but that people work in the Lord's Supper.

It's unfair to say that that's all he taught us. We were taught that it was a time of fellowship. We discussed what it meant to "proclaim the Lord's death until he comes."

"Can we use anything other than unleavened bread and grape juice?" we asked. "Why not wine instead of grape juice?" "Can you take it on other days besides Sundays?"

We asked lots of questions, good questions. But the bottom line was: nothing happens in the Lord's Supper. Well, fellowship happens (perhaps, at some minimal level). Prayer happens. It is a time for the recollection of Jesus' last hours before his death. But we don't believe that God works in any particular way during the communion.

And so our understanding of these two important events, baptism and the Lord's Supper, vary greatly. We believe God works in baptism, but that people work in the Lord's Supper. Most of my life, I have not questioned this distinction. It hasn't been that big of a deal, I suppose. Now I think it is a matter of great importance for the church.

How we came to this view is critical to our understanding. It should cause us to rethink what we have done and taught, and, perhaps, it will lead to a healthier view of both baptism and the Lord's Supper—those Christian activities that the world finds so abnormal, so strange.

The History of Our Perspectives

Most traditions within Christendom would call baptism and the Lord's Supper *sacraments*. It's not a word I'm particularly fond of or advocate. But it is useful as a backdrop for this discussion. Literally, *sacrament* means an act of consecration, an oath of allegiance, a solemn obligation. It is a pledge similar to what a soldier might make binding him in obedience to his superiors.

The word *sacraments* was introduced as the Latin successor to the Greek word *mysterion*. And though *mysterion* was never used in this way in the New Testament, the medieval church used "sacraments" to refer to seven special activities in which (it was believed) God mediated grace: baptism, confirmation, the Lord's Supper, ordination, marriage, penance, and anointing (or healing). In these, God was seen to work in extraordinary ways, enabling the recipients to encounter Jesus. In the words of one contemporary Catholic book on the sacraments, "these encounters pledge grace to us as if we had met Jesus on the roads of Galilee."[1]

In the sixteenth century, the Protestant Reformers argued that there were not seven sacraments but two: baptism and the Lord's Supper. And there was considerable discussion as to how or whether these were avenues through which God mediated grace. In general, Martin Luther and John Calvin agreed that, in some sense, the sacraments of baptism and the Lord's Supper imparted grace to the recipients, that there were spiritual benefits. Huldrich Zwingli, the influential Swiss reformer, disagreed. The sacraments were pledges, or more accurately, signs that pointed to a greater reality. They served as a kind of visual aid reminding the worshipers of what God had done for them.

Of these two sacraments, the greatest controversy among the reformers occurred over the Lord's Supper, or Eucharist. Much of the discussion centered around the meaning of Jesus' words of institution: "This is my body," "This is my blood." What did Jesus mean when he said "this *is*" my body and blood? For centuries, the medieval church took him very literally: if Jesus said, "This is my body," then in some sense it must actually *be* his body.

Out of that assumption, the Roman Catholic church, using arguments from Aristotelian metaphysics, came to teach that during the priest's prayer of consecration, the bread and the wine actually became the body and blood of Jesus. While the bread and wine still looked and tasted like bread and wine (the so-called "accidents" or appearance of the elements remained the same), their "substance" genuinely changed into the flesh and blood of Jesus. (After all, Jesus did say, "This is my body.") This doctrine was called "transubstantiation": the substance was transformed into Jesus Christ in the flesh.

All of the reformers argued against this doctrine. Its abuses had been numerous. The Eucharist had become a rite filled with superstition and magic. Few people were partaking any more, not feeling worthy to eat the literal flesh and drink the literal blood of Jesus. The cup was being withheld from the members out of fear that they might spill the "blood" of Christ.

For most, the sacramental moment became the "elevation of the host" where the bread was held high after it was blessed and the people gazed upon it. In many places, this event replaced actual participation in the Supper.

But while all the reformers firmly rejected this doctrine, they were considerably divided (and often acrimonious) about what they thought happened in the Lord's Supper. Luther was closest to the Catholic position. While he denied that the substance of the elements was actually changed (a heresy he laid at the feet of the old "billy goat" Aristotle—against whose philosophy he strongly argued), he did believe that somehow, mysteriously, the body of Jesus Christ was present with the bread and wine (or as later Lutherans said, "in, with, and under"). His real presence was there, and participants actually encountered in some genuine way the body of Jesus Christ.

Calvin objected. The body of Christ, he said, was not here; it was at the right hand of God. Christ's body was in no way transported down to us during the Eucharist. Rather, the worshipers were transported (spiritually) to heaven where Christ was. How this happened or in what sense, of course, was a mystery. In this way, Calvin said, the worshipers actually encountered Jesus, but not bodily in the bread and wine.

Zwingli's beliefs were considered the most radical. He said that when Jesus proclaimed to his disciples, "this is my body," he meant, "this signifies my body." The body of Christ was not actually present. The Lord's Supper was not a time to experience or encounter Christ, but to *remember* him. It was a memorial, a time of recollection of the death of Jesus. More than that, it was a pledge of our faithfulness to him.

Unquestionably, Zwingli's views on worship, and specifically the Lord's Supper, dominated the so-called Reformed tradition (initially the Swiss Reformation, Calvin's and Zwingli's followers). Zwingli's position on the Lord's Supper was the prevailing view of the eighteenth century Scottish Presbyterians who were direct spiritual descendants of Zwingli (through John Knox, who lived in exile among the Swiss Reformed churches for several years in the 1550s). Through this and other Reformed sources, many Americans adopted this position. And it especially characterizes the understanding of many American evangelical churches.

God Encounters Us in
Our Remembering

But, I believe, Zwingli took a wrong turn. He may have done it for right reasons, but the negative effects have been significant. Zwingli was right that Jesus' words of institution, "This is my body," don't mean that the body of Christ is miraculously in the elements. And he was right that the Supper is a memorial. But he was wrong in understanding the meaning of *memorial*.

Zwingli's view of remembrance was thoroughly Hellenistic. To remember was to recall or recollect. To remember Christ in the Supper was to rehearse in our minds who Jesus was and what Jesus did hundreds of years ago.

But the backdrop of Jesus' words was not Hellenistic but Hebraic. In neither the Old Testament nor the New Testament is *remembrance* ever used in this western sense. To a Hebrew, to remember meant to reexperience in the present the power and effect of a past event. It was a reappropriation, not merely a recollection.

And so, as Jews celebrated the Passover, which was the immediate context of Jesus' words of institution, they did not conceive it as a time simply to recall what God did for their ancestors hundreds of years before. Rather, to this day, when the youngest son asks his father, "Why is this night different from all other nights," the father replies, "Our father was a wandering Aramean. He went into Egypt and lived there as an alien, and there he became a great nation, mighty and populous. But the Egyptians treated us harshly and afflicted us, imposing hard labor on us. We cried to the Lord, the God of our ancestors; the Lord heard our voice and saw our affliction, our toil, and our oppression. The Lord brought us out of Egypt with a mighty hand and an outstretched arm."

It was not "our ancient ancestors" whom he delivered, but "us." To remember the Passover was to reexperience fully the deliverance of the mighty hand of God. It was not simply to recall an incident that occurred many years before.

To a Hebrew, to remember meant to reexperience in the present the power and effect of a past event.

And to "do this in remembrance of me" does not mean merely to recollect the events of Jesus' death but to experience fully its present power. The same Christ who sacrificed himself for our sakes and was raised by the power of God from the dead, meets us in the eating of the bread and the drinking of the cup, not because he is contained in the elements, but because *he encounters us in our remembering.*

We Encounter God in His World, Not Ours

I believe the Bible clearly teaches that in both baptism and the Lord's Supper we encounter Jesus Christ. I believe God does something, that these are more than human actions.

That does not mean these are "sacraments" in a traditional Catholic or even Protestant sense. God's grace is not infused into the worshipers. Nor does any wave of awe overwhelm us. We cannot bring it about by creating an atmosphere of wonder (with certain arrangements of the room, aesthetic adornments, just the right music, or the reverent language of the preacher). This encounter is not just something to which we respond with chills and goosebumps. Something else occurs.

The traditional view of sacraments is that the abnormal or divine breaks into the normal, mundane world in which we live. This, I believe, is precisely what does not happen. This is not the occasional inbreaking of the Extraordinary into the ordinary, the intrusion of the Abnormal into our normal, everyday affairs. Rather, *we* live in the great abnormality. We live poles away from what our lives should be—what they were created to be.

Do you think God planned a world filled with such sin and decadence? Did God desire a world with such squalor, murder, terrorism, rage, and abuse? A world in which all of us are inextricably bound up in selfishness, greed, pettiness, and gossip?

No, this world is the abnormal one. In baptism and the Lord's Supper, we begin to participate in God's world, the normal world as he envisioned it. In the words of Vernard Eller, as we take the bread and drink from the cup, our hearts exclaim, "This is the life for which we were made; things seem familiar—right and normal—for once. Lord, we're home!"[2]

This is not some sort of magic. It doesn't grow out of superstition or a need to manipulate God to our purposes. Nor are we doing it simply because the disciples did (which creates the kind of mundane, lifeless Lord's Suppers in which many of us have participated). But, we believe, God is present. The crucified and resurrected Christ is with us still. In experiencing the crucifixion again—and again—God raises us up into the heavenlies to see a glimpse of the world as he intended it.

The Consequences of Downplaying the Cross

To show the importance of these cross-shaped events, look for a moment at the first-century church at Corinth. These Christians lived in a pluralistic world very much like our own. It was a world of greed and decadence, of human achievement and pagan excesses. And the church was greatly influenced by the prevailing values. In fact, many of the Christians were embarrassed by some of the tenets of the church's teaching. They knew that the crucifixion of Jesus would be considered especially strange in the Corinthian community. So they underplayed it. They did not talk much about the cross, about a god who relinquished his immortality, about the leader of their movement who was executed like a criminal. The leading citizens of Corinth thought such teaching foolish.

Instead, the Christians played up the things that connected with their culture: they emphasized their knowledge and their power. Their knowledge came because of their mastery of Hellenistic wisdom. They were able to integrate many of the main ideas of Christian teaching with prevailing Greek wisdom. Moreover, they were convinced that in so doing they had surpassed even Paul in understanding and, therefore, were beginning to challenge his apostolic authority over them.

The consequences of downplaying the cross and highlighting their wisdom and power were monumental.

Their power came from their spiritual gifts. And the exercise of those gifts brought considerable attention to themselves and their apparent spirituality.

But the consequences of downplaying the cross and highlighting their wisdom and power were monumental. As Paul writes his second letter to them (what we know as "1 Corinthians" [see 1 Cor. 5:9]), he confronts them with the effects of these doctrinal perversions. They were a church noted for their divisions ("I am of Paul, I am of Apollos . . .") (chaps. 1–4). In order to "fit in" with their culture, they had bowed down before the god of tolerance. In fact, they were so tolerant, they out-paganed the pagans, accepting in their church, without rebuke, a man who was having sexual relations with his stepmother (chap. 5). They were parading their personal disputes publicly among the pagans (chap. 6).

Their marriages were being affected. Some of the men assumed that having sexual relations with prostitutes would not have an impact on their marriages or their relationship with Christ (chap. 6). Others (or maybe the same ones?) thought that to be truly spiritual meant not having to have sexual relations with their wives (chap. 7). Many of them were asserting their rights, insisting on having the freedom to do what they wanted no matter the consequences (chaps. 8–10).

Their assemblies had become chaotic. Some were coming early to the community meal and not waiting for the others. Some were even getting drunk at the Lord's table (chap. 11). The ones who had the gift of speaking in tongues were arguing with those who had the gift of prophecy concerning which gift was most important (chap. 12). Some of the wives were challenging the teaching of their husbands right in the middle of the assembly (chap. 14).

In almost every paragraph of this extremely blunt letter, Paul confronts them with the effects of their teaching. The Corinthians may have prided themselves in their sophistication, their wisdom, and their power, but this was not the kind of world God intended.

God's way is the way of the cross (chap. 1). While it may appear strange to all who hear it, while it may be a stumbling block to Jews and appear utterly foolish to the Gentiles, nevertheless we will preach a Christ who was crucified. It may not appear all that wise to the great thinkers of Corinth, it may be politically unacceptable within the social circles of the city, but God's wisdom is greater than the wisdom of the world. Whether or not it appears strange, the cross of Jesus will be at the heart of the Christian witness.

The Corinthian Christians may have spent their time fighting over who was most important, they may have insisted, in the name of freedom, on doing what they wanted to do, the way they wanted to do it. They may have underplayed the teaching of the cross because it was strange to their friends and associates. But Jesus chose a different route. He walked the road of suffering. He chose the lowly positions. He was willing to sacrifice for the needs of others. He placed his concern for others above himself. This may not fit into human views of wisdom, but it is God's way.

And so, the entire Corinthian epistle is a summary of what life could be like if lived by the principle of the cross. People would be able to work with one another without rancor or divisiveness. They wouldn't live in immorality and would lovingly discipline those who do. They wouldn't publicly display their disputes before the pagans. Their marriages would be transformed into relationships of mutual care and compassion. They would be willing to relinquish their rights for the good of others. Their assemblies would become times of encouragement and mutual nurture. They would be able to look at death victoriously and anticipate the glorious resurrection to come. And they would be inspired to look beyond themselves in order to provide for the needs of others.

The cross may be embarrassing, strange, even scandalous. It certainly appears foolish to the world. Nevertheless, let this be your identity: you are people of the cross. You live crucified lives. Give up your lives for each other's sake as Jesus gave up his life for you.

Now it is possible to understand Paul's discussion of the Lord's Supper. Every time you share in the cup, you share in the blood of Christ. Every time you partake of the loaf, you partake of Christ's body (1 Cor. 10:16).

For I received from the Lord what I also handed on to you, that the Lord Jesus on the night when he was betrayed took a loaf of bread, and when he had given thanks, he broke it and said, "This is my body that is for you. Do this in remembrance of me." In the same way he took the cup also, after supper, saying, "This cup is the new covenant in my blood. Do this, as often as you drink it, in remembrance of me." For as often as you eat this bread and drink the cup, you proclaim the Lord's death until he comes. (1 Cor. 11:23–26 NRSV)

Renewed by the Crucified Christ

There is a fresh wind blowing in our midst. I believe that it is the breath of God renewing and revitalizing us. Many churches are experiencing a resurgence of praise and worship, of commitment and discipleship. Christians are reexamining and strengthening their faith. In many places, individual Bible study is on the rise; small groups devoted to fellowship, study, worship, and evangelism are burgeoning, and more and more people are participating in the spiritual disciplines of prayer and fasting.

This does not mean, however, that every attempt at renewal is from God or that every change is constructive. Many see this time of renewal as an opportunity to exert what they see as their freedom, believing that now they get to do what they want to do in worship. Some are pushing for major innovations in style and format. And in several congregations, this has created considerable strain.

Some of my friends assume that if only they could have worship teams or drama groups, then congregational worship would be better. Other of my friends insist that no changes should be made from the worship styles crystallized in the 1950s, that any modifications of that would simply be "change for change's sake."

I think both positions miss the point. Renewal will not occur merely because of extensive, if well meaning, worship innovations. Nor will right worship occur because I insist on doing it in the way that is most comfortable to me. Authentic worship will take place only when we lay our lives at the foot of the cross. What is most needed is neither changing worship nor keeping it the same. Rather, our churches need Christians who will place themselves under the shadow of the crucified Christ.

If we lived crucified lives, we would not insist on our own way but would aggressively seek the best interests of others. Our conversations would exhibit the concerns of Christ. Our behavior would reflect the purity of Christ. Our marriages would be transformed by the sacrifice of Christ. Our congregations would nurture the disciplines of Christ. And in our worship, we would be renewed again by the power and compassion of Christ, who was not only crucified for us on an ancient Judean hill, but who is present with us in our remembrance of him.

One Bright Chain of Loving Rite

As we gather for worship, we are able to see more clearly that sin has spoiled the world God created. God never intended that we live this way. His created order has been perverted. Each of us is going our own way. We live the way we want to live and find the justification for it. But he is not removed from the world, even in its rebellion. In fact, at the very height of our revolt, in the face of our godlessness, Christ died for us. And through his death we are reclaimed and redeemed.

At our baptism, we voluntarily sacrifice the things the world counts as most precious. We surrender the goals and lifestyles that characterize the world that is passing away. He calls us to a different way of living—virtuous, resolute, unsullied by pagan influences, holy. He desires us to live with distinctive values. In our baptism, we are empowered by his spirit to live crucified lives among people who do not know him.

In the Lord's Supper, we remember—we reexperience—the death of Jesus. God breaks in and shows us *his* world. In partaking, we not only signify Christ's body and blood, we participate in them. And we make a covenant that we will embody his sacrificial life. Week after week, we are renewed to be an alternative community, citizens of a heavenly kingdom. We take the bread and the cup, and we surrender our will to the will of Christ, and we declare that we will live out the implications of Christ's death—by Christ's power—until he comes.

As we gather for worship, we are able to see more clearly that sin has spoiled the world that God created.

It seems certain to me that many of our Christian teachings and practices will always appear strange to the world. Our society will never understand the nature and power of the cross of Jesus. Nevertheless, it is under the shadow of that cross that we will stand. It is by its standards that we will walk. And it is by its power that we will live in the midst of a world that has lost its way.

In the words of George Rawson, the worshiping community exclaims: *By Christ redeemed, in Christ restored*—the power of his crucifixion is present with us again. *We keep the memory adored,* as we are confronted by the cross in the eating of the bread and the drinking from the cup. *And show the death of our dear Lord, until he come!* Then this extraordinary reflection: *And thus that dark betrayal night, with the last advent we unite. . . .* By God's divine hand, the cross and the second coming of Christ are brought together. But how? *By one bright chain of loving rite. . . .* Week after week, as we participate in this sacred ritual, our hearts are quickened, our commitments are made sure, our souls are cleansed, our faith is emboldened, and our wills surrender to the crucified and resurrected Christ, *until he come!*

---

1. Michael Scanlon and Anne Theresa Shields, *And Their Eyes Were Opened: Encountering Jesus in the Sacraments* (Ann Arbor: Word of Life, 1976), 12.

2. Vernard Eller, *In Place of Sacraments: A Study of Baptism and the Lord's Supper* (Grand Rapids: Eerdmans, 1972), 14. I am indebted to Eller for these insights.

MAX LUCADO

◆

See What the Lord Has Done

Worship and Evangelism

CHAPTER SEVEN

When it came down to it, Milo Hamilton just spoke his heart.

After months of pondering, he ad-libbed the big call.

Though he'd scripted the moment, spontaneity took over.

Once, maybe twice, in an announcer's career, he will have the opportunity to say something immortal. Unforgettable. Placed in front of the microphone at the right moment in history, his words will forever travel with the event.

Milo had his opportunity. He was the radio voice of the Atlanta Braves. He had manned the microphone for the Cubs and the White Sox before moving to Atlanta. And what a fortuitous move it was. The year was 1974, the year Hank Aaron hit his 715th career home run. The home run that broke Babe Ruth's record.

The baseball world could see it coming. The countdown had begun months before. And Milo Hamilton knew he would be there to announce it.

Sports broadcasters seldom have the privilege of preparing for such a moment. When Bobby Thomson knocked the home run that won the 1951 World Series, Russ Hodges screamed, "The Giants win the pennant! The Giants win the pennant! The Giants win the pennant!" Over and over and over, finally interrupting the repetition with, "I don't believe it! I don't believe it! I don't believe it!"

Describing the epic home run of Ted Williams in his last time at bat in the majors, Curt Gowdy indulged in the same cadence, "It's got a chance! It's got a chance! And it's gone!" Unplanned and unrehearsed. Usually that's how it is in broadcasting.

Milo Hamilton, however, had a chance to prepare. So did Phil Rizutto, the voice of the Yankees in 1961. He was at the mike when Roger Maris hit his record-breaking sixty-first home. Did he prepare? You be the judge. "Holy cow!" he yelled. "That's gonna be it."

Hamilton had intentions of being a bit more creative. He planned to wax eloquent as Aaron circled the bases, using each base as a marker along the way. ("He steps on first . . . the first to hit 715 home runs . . . he steps on second, breaking a record held for two decades . . .")

As for the proclamation at the crack of the bat, Hamilton planned to crown Aaron as the new home-run king. "Baseball has a new home-run king! It's Henry Aaron!" What it lacked in drama, it made up for in brevity.

But when the great moment came, spontaneity took over. Aaron circled the bases too quickly for the oratory, and Hamilton was too startled to say anything but, "It's gone! Baseball has a new home-run champion."

No harm done. It's hard to know what you are going to say when you see the impossible. But one thing is sure. You are going to say something. Silence is not an option. The wonder is not kept a secret. The witness will speak. Testimonials will be shared. Whether ad-libbed or prepared—it's only natural to tell the world when the incredible has occurred.

That must have been how the woman at the well felt.

No, she didn't have a microphone, and she hadn't seen a home run. She had seen much more. She had seen the Messiah. And when she did, she knew she had to speak. Silence was not an option. She ran so fast to tell the news that she left her water jar at the well.

Let me remind you of her story.

If you'd seen her walking toward the well that day in Samaria, here is what you would have witnessed: a weary woman trudging up a dusty hill at high noon.

If you'd lived in the nearby village, here's what you would have known: She has failed at marriage. Not once, not twice—but five times.

If you'd been in on the gossip, here's what you would have heard: She's had five husbands and the guy she's with now won't marry her.

Had you grown up in the village, here's what you would have been taught: Watch yourself, or you'll grow up to be like her.

But had you watched Jesus as he talked to her, here's what you would have witnessed: the gentle physician stitching up a tattered heart.

Here's what happened.

She comes to the well at noon. Why? Why not at dawn as did the other women? Doesn't make sense unless it was the other women she sought to avoid. Maybe the heat of the sun was more bearable than the heat of their gossip. So she comes to the well at noon.

But today she's not alone. A stranger sits at the base of the well, legs outstretched, eyes closed. Face moist from the heat. The woman looks around and sees no one else. When she looks back, his eyes are open and looking at her. Embarrassed, she turns away.

He stands and asks her for a drink of water.

Her response is salty with distrust, "You are a Jew and I am a Samaritan woman, how can you ask me for a drink?" (John 4:9). The woman has reason to be cautious. She knows what men really mean when they ask for favors. The wall is up. Jesus removes the top brick.

"If only you knew the free gift of God and who it is asking you for water, you would have asked him, and he would have given you living water" (v. 10).

No lecture. No speeches. No homilies on how far he had come to help. No finger-pointing at her past. None of that. Just an appeal. An appeal for trust.

"If only you knew . . . "

"If only you knew that I have come to help and not condemn. If only you knew that tomorrow will be better than today. If only you knew the gift I have brought: eternal life—endless, tearless, graveless life . . . if only you knew."

The woman is slow to trust.

"The well is very deep and you have nothing to get water with. Are you greater than Jacob, our father, who gave us this well?" (vv. 11–12).

Shrewd this woman. Streetwise. She knows what galls a Jew. She calls Jacob "our father." Any Jew worth his sandal won't stand for that. Samaritans are half-breeds. Rotten apples on the family tree. By calling Jacob "our father," she was claiming kinship with Jesus. If this man were like the other Jews she knew, he'd be off in a huff and she'd have her well to herself.

But he wasn't. And she didn't.

The high sun casts short shadows of the two. She still holds her jug. He still holds her attention. "Whoever drinks the water I give will never be thirsty. The water I give will become a spring of water gushing up inside that person, giving eternal life" (v. 14).

The words connect. She pilgrims a parched desert. Face furrowed. Eyes searching. Endless sage and sorrow. Every oasis a wavy mirage. Five times love pledged. Five times love failed. She's been thirsty so long.

"Sir, give me the water so I'll never be thirsty again" (v. 15).

Now she removes a few bricks. Her distrust still great, her desperation still greater . . . she's willing to take the risk.

So is Jesus. But one wall still stands. There is one obstacle remaining. The teacher gently invites her to dismantle it. "Go get your husband and come back here" (v. 16).

She winces at the words. *My husband? My husband! I don't want to talk about my husband. Talk to me about water. About eternal life. Talk to me about anything but the part of my life that hurts the most.*

She looks into the eyes of this Jew and wonders what is behind them. *He is different. He doesn't treat me like other Jews. He doesn't look at me like other men.* She could change the subject. She could ignore the question. She could lie. But none of that seems right. So she removes what remains of the wall between them.

"I have no husband"(v. 17).

Read slowly Jesus' response. "You are right to say you have no husband. Really you have had five husbands, and the man you live with now is not your husband. You have told the truth."

That's all Jesus seeks. That we tell the truth. That we come out of hiding. An encounter with Christ is midnight at the masquerade. Time to remove the mask.

And so she does. With the walls down and the mask off, she entrusts him with her deepest yearning. "Sir, I see that you are a prophet. Our ancestors worshiped on this mountain, but you Jews say that Jerusalem is a place where people must worship"(vv. 19–20).

Don't misinterpret what the woman is doing with this question.

She's not avoiding Jesus; she's inviting Jesus. She's not closing up; she's opening up. She's escorting this teacher up to the edge of the darkest cave in her world and asking him if he has a candle.

Let me tell you where I really hurt, she is saying. *Let me tell you what keeps me awake at night. Not the rejection. I'm used to being lonely. I can stand having no husband. What I cannot stand is not knowing where God is. Can you tell me?*

Pain distills the deep questions.

Look at Jesus. Weary no longer. Look at his eyes, dancing with energy. Thirst disappears. Fatigue is forgotten. He lifts the jar off the shoulder of the woman and motions her to sit down. And there in the shadow of the well of Sychar, to a rejected woman, God explains the mystery of worship.

He tells her that a day is coming when the place of worship won't make any difference. A time is coming and has come when the *where* and the *when* of worship will not matter. What matters is the heart.

Had the disciples heard this, the words would have sailed over their heads. Had the Pharisees heard this, they would have gathered stones to attack. Had I heard this, I would have looked at Jesus and said, "Can you repeat that?"

Finding God seeking us. This is worship.

But when the woman heard this—she smiled. She knew what Jesus meant, and she told him. "I know that the Messiah is coming. When the Messiah comes he will explain everything to us" (v. 25).

The moment is magical.

It's Lindbergh spotting the land through the clouds. It's Handel pounding on his piano the final measure of "The Messiah." It's Michelangelo stepping back and looking for the first time at his completed David. "Speak," he urged it.

It's the Messiah finding a Messiah-seeker.

It's the definition of worship. A hungry heart finding the Father's feast. A searching soul finding the Father's face. A wandering pilgrim spotting the Father's house. Finding God. Finding God seeking us. This is worship. This is a worshiper.

Of all the places to meet one—a well in the desert? No cathedral. No stained glass. No homily. No icons. No candles or choirs.

Of all the people to be one—a five-time divorcée? One hand hanging to the bottom rung of the social ladder. Everything about her was wrong. The wrong past. The wrong race. The wrong gender. The wrong marriage. But one thing about her was right. Her honesty. She had an honest heart.

Look at these two! She's a washed up barmaid in a one-stoplight town. He's the creator of the universe and the sustainer of the stars. But she's convinced that God's too good to leave her alone. And he's convinced that she's too good to live without. So he pulls back the curtain.

"I am the Messiah."

She wants to see God. God wants to be seen.

She was honest with him about her past. Now he's honest with her about his. She entrusted him with her longing. He entrusts her with his identity. She wants to see God. God wants to be seen.

Had I been an angel, I would have objected. Had I been a part of the heavenly host, I would have spoken up, "Not here Jesus! This is not the time, and she is certainly not the person. Wait till you get a crowd. Wait till you get an audience with a king or a priest or somebody important. Don't dump all your pearls out in a pawn shop."

But as far as Jesus was concerned—this was the right time. She was the right person.

We know she is the right person by what she does next. She drops her jug and runs as fast as her feet will take her back to the city. "Come and see a man who told me everything I ever did. Do you think he might be the Christ?" (v. 29).

In the passing of a few minutes, she goes from being a cynic to a convert to a missionary. What happened? Two things. She saw Jesus. And she saw Jesus seeing her. When she saw him and saw his love . . . she told her story.

Like Milo Hamilton, her announcement was unprepared and unrehearsed. But unlike Hamilton's, hers was uninhibited. She left her heavy jug at the well and raced back to the village and announced, "Could it be that he is the Messiah?"

When one has seen the impossible, silence is not an option.